How to Build a Positive Attitude

I'm not Missing Anything

How to Build a Positive Attitude and KEEP the Darn Thing!!

by Charlie Adams

HOW TO BUILD A
POSITIVE ATTITUDE
AND KEEP THE DARN THING!!

10 9 8 7 6 5 4 3 2

ISBN 978-0-9859377-7-5

Published by
CORBY BOOKS
A Division of Corby Publishing, LP
P.O. Box 93
Notre Dame, In 46556
www.corbypublishing.com
(574) 784-3482

Manufactured in the United States of America

Introduction

IN ALL THE YEARS I have been delivering motivational programs, the topic most requested by meeting planners all over the world relates to attitude. We all know how important it is to have, but it sure can be hard to keep a positive attitude all the time, huh?

This book is filled with tools and insights on how to be as positive as possible. I was in television news for a quarter of a century. Whether I was anchoring the morning news or anchoring the sports, I put a positive spin on things. Viewer response was so strong that management also made me a positive news reporter. I put together features on people with amazingly positive attitudes and, over time, learned from them how to stay positive and content almost all of the time. In this book you will find their secrets to building and keeping a positive attitude.

This observation from a Midwest business owner speaks volumes about the importance of a positive attitude: "If you list the ten most important characteristics you want in an employee, eight of the ten relate to attitude. The person with the right attitude will learn the skills and the system. Someone with a poor attitude is far less likely to succeed, regardless of their skills or system." (Phil Linden, Linden's Propane, Lagrange, Ohio)

I wrote this book because of the response to the "How to Build a Positive Attitude and KEEP the Darn Thing!!" two-hour and half-day seminars that many corporate, school and church audiences have been able to experience. For many years I have delivered a motivational keynote called "Stoke the Fire Within" at all kinds of conferences. Because many were day-long conferences, meeting planners asked me to develop a two-hour session called a "breakout session." Attendees have the choice of picking the "breakout" they would like throughout that day. Well, they would go by the room and see "How to Build a Positive Attitude and KEEP the Darn Thing!!" and just pour in. I did it in Chicago one time at an Insurance Conference and so many people came in the room that I was backed to a wall. The next week in Fairbanks the same thing happened. This was before the recession! What it told me was that people want to pick up a few tools to be more positive.

That's what this book is about. I love the positive attitude books that have quotes from famous people, but I wanted to make this book different so I sought out how normal, everyday-life people like you and me try to build and keep positive attitudes. Here is an example of what you will see throughout this book:

> Charlie, we all chase happiness, I think—we all seek it. But "Where do you find it?" is a great question. Look at the successful athletes and movie stars with the expensive cars, big homes, toys, plenty of money, thin bodies...yet many struggle with drug and alcohol abuse, suicides, broken relationships. I feel circum-

stantial things and events—cars, vacations, etc.—have a short-lived shelf life in overall happiness. It will boost happiness but then we go back to our "set point." How we think—our self-talk—and how we behave impact on our happiness or lack of it. So, if a person can find the things that fill them up, [that is what will] make them happy—not buying stuff, or eating or drinking, but the things that bring peace to their heart. Take the time to do more of those things and be aware of how you talk to yourself. At the end of the day you are the only one who has the power to change anything about yourself or your life. We must stop looking to others or things to do this for us.

– Mary Zeisz Dunfee, realtor

It is my hope that this book can be life changing for you. The format is basically to have a chapter on attitude tools and then a chapter on someone with a powerful positive attitude. People learn from stories, so there are lots of stories in here. I have interviewed several thousand people about attitude over my half century of life, and have poured their insights into this book. You will see places for you to write and reflect here. I want this book to be a helpful resource for you so that you can be as positive and on fire about life as possible!

– Charlie Adams

Contact Information for
Charlie Adams Motivation:
Office Direct Line: 574 807 2279
Main email: charlie@stokethefirewithin.com
Websites: www.charlieadamsmotivation.com
www.stokethefirewithin.com
facebook.com/charlieadamsmotivation
twitter.com/Positive Charlie@PositiveCharlie

— 1 —

Initial Spin

I AM GOING TO START THIS BOOK with a tool that I have used for years to help make something positive out of everything that happens in life. For many years I have hosted inspirational group travel trips for Edgerton's Travel. On one such trip, an elderly lady told me that she had recently become married for the first time. She was in her late 70s. "I never looked at myself as an old maid all those years when no one asked me to get married," she told me. "I always looked at myself as undiscovered treasure."

Wow! That is a positive way of looking at things. Another time I was in Columbia on a bus going on an excursion. The road was very bumpy—I mean we were bouncing up and down in our seats. It was starting to make me a bit negative. Then the guide said, "Don't think of it as bumpy. Think of it as a…massage!"

Those are examples of spins we can put on things. And then there is "Initial Spin," which is very important in building and keeping a positive attitude.

During WWII, a family in England raced to their bomb shelter when the Nazi planes came for another raid. From inside the shelter, they could hear the bombs dropping from the sky and feel the explosions all around them; and, when they came out, they saw that their house was gone. What remained was a crater. The father used initial spin: "We have always wanted to have a home with a basement. Now we can have one!" By taking that perspective from the start, he launched a positive approach to the considerable work that lay ahead of them. I put this same technique to use a number of years ago when my house was hit by a tornado. A massive beech tree was uplifted and dropped on the roof, causing all kinds of damage. I knew there would be months of clean-up work, but took the initial spin of: "I needed a new roof and now I'll get one." (Just don't tell the insurance guy I took that approach, since they paid for it.)

There have been many cases where property devastation has led to people coming away with a more positive attitude. I once read of a church near me that suffered significant fire damage. The pastor immediately told the local media that he thought God would bring many positives from the challenge. Indeed, the neighboring community rallied around the church. Many people started attending who never had before, even though they lived nearby. Their youth group grew as a church band developed, which they called "After the Fire." When the building was finally repaired, they saw their attendance grow significantly.

Speaking of churches, there once was a couple sitting near a family with a crying baby. The husband became irritated and muttered something about the noise. The wife took the initial spin of: "Be thankful that we have families with young children...some churches are struggling to get them in their buildings."

And when David first saw Goliath, he could have said, "He is SO big!" and shuddered in fear. Or, he could have said, "He is so big that I cannot miss!"

Two salesmen from different shoe companies arrived at a faraway island where those who lived there did not wear shoes. The first salesman took the initial spin that focused on the negative: "They don't wear shoes here. I am coming home." The second one took the positive initial spin: "They don't wear shoes here! Send shoes!"

When someone close to us dies it is obviously a very hard time. Though there is grieving, I always try to take the initial spin from the Dr. Seuss quote: "Don't be sad it's over. Be glad it happened." Yes, there is sadness that they are gone but, when you think about all the good things that happened when they were there, you become grateful to have experienced those things.

You can use humor as an initial spin even in the most serious of scenarios. I delivered "How to Build a Positive Attitude and KEEP the Darn Thing!!" for the staff of the University of Alaska-Fairbanks. While at the seminar they talked with great pride about their national-championship-winning Rifle team which was coached by Dan Jordan. When Dan was a student-athlete there (and one of the best rifle competitors in the world), he had a serious fall while rock climbing. He fell and crashed to the rocks below. It was so serious that he is partially paralyzed to this day, yet when it happened he was able to spin some humor. When paramedics got there and rushed to his side one of them asked, "Are you allergic to anything!?"

"Yeah," Jordan answered. "Rocks!"

With a positive attitude, Jordan became a Paralympics rifle athlete and remains the only person to shoot at a world-class level with both the able-bodied and Paralympics athletes. By staying positive and focusing on what he could do, Jordan became head Rifle coach at the University and guided them to three national championships in his first three years as coach. He was named national coach of the year for three straight years. Ironically, he became the president of The Optimist (Civic) Club in Fairbanks! I remember being up in Fairbanks one time and happening to catch an article on him. In it, he simply said that he tried to have as good an attitude as possible about things.

If you want a Doctorate in Initial Spin, try what the fellow in Vegas did when he was out there with his wife. She was in the shower getting ready for dinner. Now as I recall, there has been a time or two in world history when a wife has taken longer than she says she will to get ready for an evening out, so this fellow leaned his head in the bathroom and said he was taking a couple of dollars down to the roulette table. He got down there and did a double or nothing on black and won. He did another double and won. He got on a roll to beat all rolls and his money kept doubling. He got up to a couple grand. Glancing at his watch, he knew it was time to go back upstairs but figured one more roll. He put it on red and it landed on black. There went those winnings.

He got back to the room and the wife asked him how he did. He simply replied, "Oh, I lost two dollars."

When people ask me why I am so positive all the time, I tell them I have trained myself to put as positive a spin on things as possible at the initial stage they happen to me. For example, I was delivering the two-hour form of "How to Build a Positive Attitude and KEEP the Darn Thing!!" for members of the Goshen Chamber of Commerce. I had finished my 8 to 10 a.m. session and was going to listen to another speaker from 10 to noon. I went out to my car to get something and saw that the left back tire had lost much of its air. Rather than go "Aww, man!" I immediately told myself that I was thankful that I had detected it before it had gone completely flat and that I was grateful that I was downtown. I figured there had to be a tire store somewhere close. I walked back inside to the Chamber Director and asked him for a place. He told me about Monteith Tire down the road and I drove the car down there. They put it up on their rack, found a nail, patched it up and I was back sitting in the next session at 10:35 a.m.

Try to develop a habit of putting an initial positive spin on everything, especially challenges, and it will help you to keep that positive attitude!

— 2 —

Grizzly Bear Destroys Store! Owner Makes It a Positive!

THERE ARE MANY ATTITUDES that work together to make an organization or a person succeed. Of course, there is the positive attitude, but one of the most important is the "find a way" attitude or the "make the best of a bad situation" attitude!

In Alaska I once saw a remarkable example of taking a negative and making it a big positive! On our way to cross the Arctic Circle, the group I was with came across the Yukon River Café. I took the photo below of the picture they had near the front door...of a giant grizzly bear butt!

I do not know of any other business in the world that has a big picture of a grizzly's butt at the entrance to their business. But what a story there is to go with it...

In the brutal winter of 2004, the café had been boarded up. An old grizzly came by and found that two other bears had created a hole into the place. They were in there for the winter. The grizzly promptly kicked them out and took over. He then proceeded to tear the place apart, ripping the fridge and oven open to look for food. He decided that the large gift shop area would be his sleeping area and so he knocked all of the nice t-shirts and sweatshirts off the rack and slept on them and also did all his "bathroom duties" on them.

A security guard for the nearby Alaska Pipeline saw this and got word to the owner of the Yukon River Café that a bear was wreaking havoc on the place. In what is truly another story in itself, the owner and two others arrived with guns...but no key. The owner had forgotten it. Not wanting to knock in the front door and damage it, the three men (who were wearing head flashlights because the electricity had been turned off) crawled through the same hole the bears had created. Thank goodness the bear was not near the entrance. The first thing they saw were all the torn and soiled shirts.

They slowly moved through the place, eventually getting to a long hallway that had a row of showers. At the far end, two menacing eyes stared back. As it started to charge, shots rang out and down went the grizzly. As it was explained to me, in Alaska you can kill a bear when you are defending life or property.

After things settled down, the owner surveyed the extensive damage to the place. The large amount of shirts looked awful. Now, in that situation most people (including ol' motivational, positive-attitude Charlie here) would have said, "Get those shirts to the dumpster."

Not the owner. He had them thoroughly washed over and over to where there was no longer a bad smell.

When the warm weather arrived and tourists started coming through, word got around about the bear that had torn the place apart. The owner took every one of those shirts and sweatshirts and put them back on the rack, with a sign that read "Bear-ly Worn."

Every one of them sold—it didn't matter if they had bear stains all over them or ripped sleeves. Consumers gobbled them up. The owner made such a profit that it helped with the costs of repairing the rest of the place!

That's the "find a way" attitude. That's the "let's make the most of this situation" attitude. That's being positive!

— 3 —

The Four Needs We All Have

THIS CHAPTER IS GOLD when it comes to something that can help you to be content in life. Sure, we want to be happy and positive, but the real key is to learn how to be content and filled with joy.

As mentioned earlier, in my television-news days I spent a considerable number of years (1988–2006) at the CBS affiliate in South Bend, where part of my job was to cover Notre Dame Football. Lou Holtz was the head football coach there for ten years (1986–96). During that time, I interviewed him hundreds of times and gained tremendous insights from him on attitude and success. Besides having success as a coach, Holtz was in demand as a motivational speaker. After retiring as a football coach, Holtz came back to South Bend and delivered a motivational talk at the annual Notre Dame Football Banquet. It was during that talk that he shared the "Four Needs" we all have in life. If we meet these needs, then we will be content and positive.

(1) Something Positive to Do/A Purpose

Let's approach this first from what we do professionally. Our positive attitude is affected greatly by what we do in our jobs. If you "have to go to work" then chances are you will be negative. But if you find the purpose in your profession, then you "get to go to work" and sometimes you "can't wait to get to work" because of how you are helping others in life.

Here are some examples of finding the purpose in your life. FedEx founder Fred Smith has told his drivers that they aren't just driving trucks around every day. No, in those trucks could be a machine part that is critical to getting an assembly line back on track. In those trucks could be a medical part that is vital to helping a person recover from a health challenge. From that perspective, those drivers have a purpose and their attitude can't help but be more positive.

Three workers were cutting stone. When asked what they were doing, the first answered, "I am cutting stone." The second said, "I am making a wall." The third replied, "I am building a cathedral." The third one had truly found purpose in his work.

I remember taking two of my children to a local minor-league baseball game. The game started at two and we got there very early. They said we had to wait about fifteen more minutes because the ballpark was being used for a private party for a local company. As we stood outside the gates, I realized the company inside was Elkhart Brass. They make innovative fire-fighting equipment. They had brought all of their employees to the ballpark for a Sunday afternoon social gathering to show appreciation for them. As it wound down and the park was about to be opened to the public, I heard their company leader take the microphone and speak to the workers. As he thanked them, he reminded them that each day they came to work they were making equipment that kept fire fighters safer and helped them to put out fires faster. I vividly remember thinking to myself, "What a purpose in a job!" Not long after that I read a local magazine story on a successful real estate agent named Jan Lazzara. In the article she stated that what kept her on fire was that she was not just helping people to buy and sell houses. She was helping them find HOMES. That gives her powerful purpose each day.

I was in the gym working out one day and had a deep conversation with the lady next to me about finding meaning in work. I said that someone who worked at a fast-food restaurant would probably struggle with finding meaning in their work because the food was not a positive thing for the customers. She corrected me by saying that someone working there could focus on being encouraging and pleasant to customers while looking to give a warm smile to that person who seemed down.

In his book *Authentic Happiness*, there is a story by the author Martin Seligman about when he visited the hospital and was in the room of a friend who was in a coma. There was a ward orderly in the room who was focused on achieving a task. Now, in the scheme of doctors and nurses you would think ward orderly would be pretty far down in the pecking order. To some it might be, but not to this man. He had a purpose. He was fixing up the paintings and flowers so they were positioned just right in the room. Seligman asked him what he was doing.

"My job. I'm an orderly here, but you see I'm part of the team responsible for the health of these patients. Even though Mr. Miller hasn't been conscious since he arrived, when he does wake up I want to make sure he sees beautiful things right away."

The orderly was able to find a deeper purpose in his job, beyond what others would think of as mundane orderly tasks. I bet he couldn't wait to get to work so that he could do things to help patients. His attitude had to be so positive compared to the person who looked at their shift that week and thought, "Well, I'm working 2 to 11 today…"

Did he come to that realization of his own accord, or was it a leader who inspired him to see the import of his work? We don't know the answer to that question, but the question it begs you to ask yourself is, "How can I help my people to create such a positive attitude about the work that they do?"

What is the PURPOSE of your work?

____

____

____

____

____

____

Another word to use here is "meaning." Viktor Frankl wrote *Man's Search for Meaning* in 1946. In 1991, the Library of Congress and the Book-of-the-Month Club listed that book as one of the ten most influential books in the U.S. The book is about Frankl's experience in Nazi concentration camps as a Jewish psychiatrist. He writes about his observation that what separated those who lived and those who died in those camps was "meaning." For example, there were two men there who were giving up on life. What Frankl did was help them find their meaning, a purpose to go on. With one man it was his son, who lived in another country. For the other it was the books that he had started to write. He became determined to get out and finish them!

"In both cases," Frankl writes, "it was a question of getting them to realize that life was still expecting something from them; something in the future was expected of them. A man who becomes conscious of the responsibility he bears toward a human being who affectionately waits for him, or to an unfinished work, will never be able to throw away his life. He knows the "why" for his existence, and he will be able to bear almost any "how."

Regarding attitude, he writes: "Everything can be taken from a man but one thing, the last of the human freedoms—to choose one's attitude in any given set of circumstances, to choose one's own way."

What is the meaning of your life? What is your "why?"

In the popular movie *City Slickers*, the grizzled cowboy Curly, played by Jack Palance, has that famous mini-speech where he explains the meaning of life. While holding up a finger he says it is "one thing." The key, he says in gruff fashion, is finding out what that one thing is for you. An entire book could be dedicated to the analysis of "one thing," but it is good to take time to reflect on what that one thing is for you. Is it the pursuit of a high level position and the financial rewards that come with it? Is it making a difference in the lives of young people? Is it loving God with all your heart and soul? Is it dedicating your life to service? What is your "one thing?"

Let me take "one thing" one more step. What is it that YOU do better than anyone else in the world? It doesn't have to be something "famous" like LeBron James is the best basketball player in the world or Meryl Streep is the best actress. It could be that no one else is better at untying a knotted-up fishing line. It could be the ability to make a sick grandchild feel better. It could be making the best pancakes in the world. Let me give you mine. In hosting Edgerton's group travel trips, I have produced a 60-minute DVD documentary of the trips. I truly believe there is nothing like it in the history of travel. I take a great deal of pride in making it first class. It moves fast. It's funny, filled with interesting video angles of scenery, and enables them to always go back on their trip. I am not being prideful, but I really think there's nothing like it in group travel. I love making it for the travelers. I work my tail off on it. It's not big or famous. You don't see it on the Travel Channel. It usually goes to just fifty travelers, but there is nothing like it. That's my "one thing" as far as what is unique about me accomplishment-wise. What about you? What is your "one thing" that you do better than anybody in the whole wide world?

____

____

____

____

Okay, back to the Four Needs we have. Here is number two:

(2) Something to Hope for/Look Forward to

I was in television news for almost a quarter of a century. It can be a brutal grind that can take the most positive person and squeeze out their optimism like toothpaste out of the tube. I remember once going into the office of my boss at the time and asking her what she did to stay positive. This was a lady who had to deal with the egos of the newsroom, staffing challenges, budget issues and all kinds of things. She opened up her desk drawer and showed me a picture of the Florida condo that her family visited each March. She said when things got negative, she often opened that drawer for a quick glance and a shot of positive attitude!

As you go through your day and all of the challenges, have a list of things that you are looking forward to and think of them when negative attitudes want to set in on you. It could be things like looking forward to:

* a child coming home from college for a visit
* tickets to the big ballgame that coming weekend
* a visit from the grandkids
* your first half-marathon
* a long-awaited trip

What are some things you have to LOOK FORWARD TO?

____

____

____

____

____

The other part of this point is Something to HOPE for. "Hope" is a powerful thing when it comes to attitude. One of my great challenges in life has been the glaucoma and cataracts I have battled since my 40s. Though it has been hard, I always have hope for better treatment, medications, procedures and surgeries. When we know there is a chance for things to be better out there, then our hope is fortified. That in turn makes our attitude more positive. Rather than focusing on what can continue to go wrong, it is vital to emphasize what possibly can go right and hope for those things.

One of the things I do to stay positive is read Joyce Meyer's daily devotional during my morning quiet time. I saved this on what she said about hope:

> I define hope as "the happy anticipation of good things." You can hope for something good to happen to you by learning how to celebrate and enjoy life.
>
> Everything in life is a process in motion. Without movement and progression there is no life. As long as you live you are always heading somewhere, and you should enjoy yourself on the way. God created you to be a goal-oriented visionary. Without a vision you become bored and hopeless.
>
> But there's something about hope that makes people lighthearted and happy. Hope is a powerful spiritual force that is activated through your positive attitude. God is positive and He wants positive things to happen to you, but that probably won't happen unless you have hope and faith.

> Expect God to bring good out of every circumstance in your life. Whatever happens, trust in the Lord...and trust in the power of hope!"
>
> – *Joyce Meyer*

What are some things in your life that you HOPE FOR?

____

____

____

____

____

____

(3) Someone to Love

This is powerful. We are put on this earth to love other people. When you get up each day and know that there are people out there that you love and that you mean something to, that will make your attitude more positive. As in the first point here, it also gives you PURPOSE because you know they are counting on you. This could be your wife or husband, significant other, siblings, nieces, nephews, grandkids, friends, co-workers and on and on. When they see that you are positive then it can have a tremendous impact on their attitude towards life. Write down three people whose lives you feel you make a positive impact on, and why:

____

____

____

(4) Something to Believe in

As Lou Holtz shared these four points, he made this one a point of emphasis. Holtz talked about belief in God and the importance and value of faith. Here is a letter that Holtz wrote to Bishop Robert Baker in 2000, when Holtz was in his second season as head football coach at the University of South Carolina. His first team had gone 0-11, but his second team was having much better success.

> Faith may be the most important ingredient that we possess in order to achieve tranquility in our lives. To me, faith is believing when you have no proof. People will often say, "Show me the proof, and I will believe." My answer is when you want proof that is not faith. That is fact. I credit the nuns and priests who have influenced my thinking during my formative years at St. Aloysius in East Liverpool, Ohio, for this attitude. It never ceases to amaze me how people tend to go through their life without faith. To me, you either have faith or, quite often, you will be filled with despair. I, like so many other people, worry needlessly. As I mature, I now see that the only thing worth losing sleep over is our salvation. Nothing else in our life is really relevant.
>
> *– Lou Holtz*

When I was in television news, I was responsible for a weekly feature called "the Athlete of the Week." Viewers and high school coaches would submit nominees. In interviewing these young people, I found them to be very respectful, bright, content, humble and outgoing. For one entire year we added the question of, "What does faith mean in your life?" We found out that over 95% of the young people were strong in their faith and almost all were in the youth group at their church. They had learned to have a healthy respect for their parents and elders. That is why I am a strong supporter of youth groups at churches. Who says teens have to have issues? I didn't when I was growing up. I was happy and content all through school. I believe a big reason why was that I was heavily involved in my youth group and I hung around those kids.

Over the years Dave Krider has asked me to speak each October to the Fellowship of Christian Athletes chapter he heads up in LaPorte, Indiana. They will have sessions where 60 to 70 high school student-athletes jam into someone's house on a weekday night to sing, have fellowship and hear a speaker. In many cases, kids there have met and started dating. Dave told me once that over the 30 years their chapter has been together they have had 12 cases where kids that met each other in there or that had both been through FCA had become married. All 12 marriages are still going strong. That's a 100% success rate of marriage!

My point in this book is not to be all preachy, but I have learned over the years that faith has a huge correlation to a positive attitude and a life of contentment and joy. I think what holds a lot of people back is that they have had a bad experience with someone or something in church and they have "had it" with going back. In many cases they had something happen with a hypocritical person and it soured them on faith. Yes, there are those folks out there and they can be maddening to some, but most folks are in church because they know they have flaws and are grateful for God's grace and want to be better, not because they want to point out your flaws.

I do Talks for corporate, school and church audiences and I can tell you that by far the warmest feeling I get is when I am at some church getting ready to speak. Another thing that is interesting is that I usually use video clips in my presentations. I am not tech savvy so I always have their people help me. I usually have challenges with corporate and school audiences with things working right, but I have never had any issue in a church. There is always someone with that gift to run things and a sweet spirit. It always goes seamlessly. There is simply a peace there…

Besides faith in God, this also means believing in yourself. The book *The Power of Positive Thinking* by Dr. Norman Vincent Peale is one of the greatest and biggest-selling attitude books in history. It stayed on the *New York Times* bestseller list for 186 straight weeks. The very first words of the book are: "Believe in yourself!" Something or someone to believe in also means believing in what your company and organization stands for in their work. It means believing in your community, your school, your club.

Write about the top five things you BELIEVE IN:

While these Four Needs (Something positive to do/ a purpose, Something to look forward to, Someone to love, and Something to believe in) are important to our having a positive attitude, one thing that can lead to a negative attitude is "Someday Isle." That's the place you want to go to, but you never do, and you end up frustrated or negative. It's things like "Someday I'll start that fitness program," or "Someday I'll start eating better," or "Someday I'll reach out to that person that I had that falling out with and make things better." Someday Isle is a good place to go to be nothing, do nothing, and to get negative.

I wanted to end this chapter with a powerful contribution from Mike O'Neill:

> Charlie, I think it is important not to get stuck in the "I'll be happy when" mode. I'll be happy when I get that new house, I'll be happy when I get that new job, I'll be happy when I lose weight.... The problem is you are unhappy until you meet those goals and with that mindset you will be unhappy then too. I have always loved the Sheryl Crow song lyric: "It's not having what you

want. It's wanting what you've got." It is easy to forget that. Believe me, I have to remind myself all the time. When my 18-year-old went off to college this year I wrote him a letter. In the letter I told him that one of the things I loved most about him was how excited he got about things. There are so many things to be excited about in this world I told him. Stay excited. Excitement and happiness are very close friends.

– *Mike O'Neill, salesman for Ciber*

— 4 —

Gracie's Broken Arm

TAKING A NEGATIVE IN LIFE and turning it into a positive is a mindset and a habit that can help you stay positive in almost any situation. How many times in life have we learned lessons about attitude from either our own children or young people that are in our lives?

My youngest daughter, Grace, broke her arm playing basketball when she was nine years old. She tripped on a foot and then a cone they had out for dribbling drills, and fell to that hard floor and broke her arm. Her passion in life is basketball. She loves it. After breaking her arm she could have become all negative and down in the dumps. Instead, she focused on the positive. She got the coolest pink cast in the history of broken arms, which was a hit at school. Instead of sitting around she was back out on the practice court a few days later with her team doing some of the drills. She said, "Dad, I can't use my right arm for a few weeks, so I am going to focus on getting better with my left arm and hand!"

That's taking a negative and turning it into a positive! In practice, she participated in the drills that she could, and when the team was playing a game, she was off to the side dribbling with her left hand. Ironically, in the sport of basketball, many players never reach their potential because they tend to favor their right arm growing up. Opponents recognize that later and defend them in a way where they make them dribble left. By working on her left as much as her right, Gracie could turn out to be a heckuva player in the game she adores. Today she can go right or left.

You never know how adversity can actually lead you to a better place. Lindsay Benko has won Olympic gold in swimming. I delivered a positive attitude seminar at the law firm where her dad worked and he told me that, when she was a young girl, she hadn't done much swimming. One day she fell out of a tree and broke an arm. The rehab included a lot of swimming. Her love of the sport started there.

At the 2000 Olympics she was a member of the USA's gold-medal-winning 4×200m freestyle relay. Four years later, at the 2004 Olympics, she earned gold swimming in the heats of the 4×200m freestyle relay and silver swimming the heats of the 4×100m freestyle relay. She also held the World Record in the short course 400 freestyle for 12 years.

It might not have happened if she hadn't tumbled from a tree....

It is sometimes amazing how a bad situation can lead to good things. I am sure you have many examples. In times of adversity, look at it as a challenge and not a threat.

Leave it to Baloo from *The Jungle Book* to sum it up best:

"You've got to accentuate the positive
Eliminate the negative
And latch on to the affirmative
Don't mess with Mister In-Between."

REFLECTION: Where in your life have you been able to take a negative situation and turn it into a positive?

___

___

___

___

___

___

___

___

___

___

— 5 —

Three Powerful Quotes

I USE THESE THREE APPROACHES to attitude every day and they make a world of difference. I share them every time I deliver the "How to Build a Positive Attitude and KEEP the Darn Thing!!" program and audiences have connected. They work!

I had the opportunity once to hear a lady named Sandra Herron from Crystal Cathedral share her life story at Evangel Heights United Methodist Church. Sandra moved just in front of the podium and chose not to bounce all over the room. She shared her many challenges and how various health issues had caused her to "explode" many times. Sandra recalled the time she was in a hospital room for weeks on end. She had no strength. All she could do was lie there. She could barely even lift her arms. Bumps on pickles could do more than she could do. As she lay there, she thought of what she could do to make a difference. She came up with an idea.

Every time a nurse or a worker would come into her

room, she would give them a radiant smile. She would hold it. Once they had finished their duties, she would mouth "Thank you" to them—no matter how trivial their task had been. It wasn't long before nurses and other workers started coming to her room for their break time. They wanted to be somewhere warm and loving.

Sandra then said something that has stayed with me ever since: **"You can celebrate life or suffer it, and it has absolutely nothing to do with your circumstances."**

That's powerful.

Many of us have trained ourselves to approach life so that we will be positive or "happy" WHEN something happens. It could be when we have that relationship or when we get that job or raise. It could be when we get better health or when the ornery boss moves on to another job.

What Sandra is saying is that we can celebrate life regardless of the circumstances. It made me think of the saying, "A happy person is not someone with a certain set of circumstances, but with a certain set of attitudes."

The second one comes from the late Zig Ziglar, who motivated hundreds of thousands of people during his life. I have used this particular quote multiple times within single days of my life and it always gets my positive attitude back on track. It is this: **"A positive attitude doesn't mean you can do anything, but a positive attitude means you can do a lot more than if you have a negative attitude."**

When delivering my seminar on attitude, I often

ask if there is a fan of the local pro sports team in the room. I then bring him or her up and find out who their favorite team is in the pro ranks. Let's say they answer the Chicago Bears. I then will say that the Bears are struggling at the wide receiver position. Next, I suggest that the person I have in the front of the room show up at the Bears' practice with a positive attitude and a determination to play receiver for the Bears. I then have the person, who is usually in their 40s and not exactly in prime shape, shuffle back and forth across the room and jump a few times. In most cases you can hear cracks and pops and heavy breathing. I then turn to the audience and ask whether they think, even with a positive attitude, that this person would make the team? A resounding "NO" follows—except for the wise guys who say yes! The point is that, even with a positive attitude, there is no way in you-know-where that person is going to make the Bears' team. I have never agreed with the "you can do anything in life." Someone who is five-foot-one-inch and slow as Christmas is not going to play for the Los Angeles Lakers. A positive attitude does not mean you can do anything but, as Zig said, a positive attitude means you can do everything better than if you have a negative attitude.

Burn that quote into your head and heart. Call on it often.

Here comes the third quote of the big three. Over the years I have visited numerous civic clubs as they have asked me to come out and share a message of how to stay positive. When I visited the Optimist Club for the first time, I was struck by the Creed they recited at the beginning of their meeting. It included this powerful observation on attitude: **"To *think* only of the *best*, to *work* only for the *best*, and to *expect* only the *best*."**

I think about that every day and put it into practice. How often do we truly think about the best? In my television news days the Sales department came up with a segment called "the Toughest Golf Holes in the Area." Viewers voted on the hardest holes and eventually I went out to play them with someone who voted on the particular hole and someone from the sponsor of the segment. I remember getting to a par-3 hole in southwestern Michigan that wasn't that long of a hole. It was probably 120 yards, BUT right after the tee box was a big body of water all the way up to the green.

Uh-oh. As a result I watched everyone go up to the tee with their 9-iron or 7-iron or whatever club AND three or four old golf balls! What were they expecting? They were expecting to come up short and hit at least one ball in the water. That's a negative approach. Why not march up there with your brand new Titleist golf ball and swing away with the firm expectation of landing the ball on the green?

"To think only of the best, to work only for the best, and to expect only the best." Why bother thinking of things that are defeating or negative? I have a whole chapter on that in this book, but strive to think only of the best. When you work at something, work towards only a first-class finished product, and expect nothing but the best.

Where I live (South Bend, Indiana), there are two examples of expecting the best. In 1974, the UCLA men's basketball team had an 88-game winning streak, the longest in the history of major college basketball. They came here to play Notre Dame. A couple of days before the game, Notre Dame coach Digger Phelps had his team practice cutting down the nets in expectation that they would upset UCLA and that there would be a huge celebration on the court. Even when they fell down by eleven points with just over three minutes to go, Phelps still expected to win. They did, rallying to upset UCLA 71-70. They then cut down the nets. In 1988, Notre Dame's football team was getting ready to play West Virginia in the national championship game. In the week's leading up to the big game, Notre Dame coach Lou Holtz assigned a senior player to each freshman. When Notre Dame had defeated West Virginia those freshmen were to carry the seniors off on their shoulders. They kept this private in practice. Was it cocky and overconfident? No, it was expecting the best. They firmly believed they would win and they did, 34-21.

Where have you not expected the best in your life?

How are you going to change your attitude in that area?

Sandra Herron says we can celebrate or suffer life. Where have you been guilty of suffering life?

Name three things, and they don't have to be "big," that you can celebrate in your life, regardless of circumstances.

— 6 —

The Most Positive People I Have Ever Interviewed

FOR YEARS DURING MY television news days at WSBT-TV (South Bend) I was a positive news reporter. Viewers would submit feature story ideas to me and I would go out and do them. I would come back to the newsroom all "aglow" and the newsroom people would say, "Uh oh, he has been around another positive attitude!"

I would bounce around the room telling everyone who would listen about the attitude of the person I had just spent half a day with. I saved their insights and eventually built part of the program "How to Build a Positive Attitude and KEEP the Darn Thing!!" from them. I have been able to inspire thousands of people from Fairbanks, Alaska, to Antigua by playing the video clips of the stories I did on these remarkable people. In this chapter I will share their valuable insights on positive attitude.

One of them was Wayne from Niles in southwestern Michigan. A viewer had emailed me to tell me about this fellow who scooted all around that small town in his wheelchair, uplifting people.

A camera man and I drove up to Niles and all over town before we eventually saw him zipping down the main street there. I ended up walking alongside him for several hours as he lifted up folks with positive statements. Wayne was born with cerebral palsy and all of its challenges. Life was not easy for him but, as we made our way around town, I took notes; and five things he said resonated loud and clear about attitude in life. Here is one of the things he told me:

"I like doing things for other people more than I like them to do it for me."

Serving and focusing on others is one of the most effective ways to have a positive attitude. By dedicating himself to uplifting others, Wayne took the focus off his challenges and filled his inner self with such a good feeling. I did hundreds of stories on people who had thrown themselves into service over the years, and I always saw an inner glow that made them so content and fulfilled in life. A great many of our Edgerton's travelers are heavily involved in service in their communities.

"I feel like if you don't put anything into life you can't really get anything out of it."

Preach it, Wayne! A lot of things in life take work, from relationships to attitudes. Wayne threw himself into each day with gusto! He didn't sit back and wait to see what life had for him.

"Another big thing is to like yourself because, if you don't like yourself, you can't expect someone else to like you either."

After being around Wayne, I could tell he really liked who he was and realized he was special, like everyone is.

"Use the ability you have and, if you can't do certain things, so what! Focus on what you have."

Wayne's limbs were obviously affected a great deal by the cerebral palsy. Rather than moping over what he could not do, Wayne set out to do what he could do!

"They don't really take the time to appreciate what they have. They're always looking for something different, so they don't take the time to appreciate what they have."

That's what Wayne told me he had observed over the years by watching healthy people. He's right. It is so easy to focus on the negative or what we don't have or someone else in our life doesn't have, that before long we get all out of whack.

Another of the most remarkable people I ever met in my TV-News days was a lady named Ril Mis. She could have been named Real Deal, because she exemplified everything a company would want in an employee.

Ril was born 3 months early, had oxygen complications, and has been blind her whole life. Instead of focusing on what she *couldn't* do in life, she focused on what she *could* do. She found work at Memorial Hospital as a dark room technician. She thought, "These are the cards I've been dealt in life. I'll play them the best I can. I'm blind. Why not work in a dark room?!"

It was 1999 when I did a TV-News inspirational story on her. Ril dutifully showed me all of the things that she did in her job. I could tell she took great pride in her work. She exemplified Excellence in her job. After showing me her daily routine, she said something that I've always remembered. "When I finish my job I go see if there's anything I can do for anyone else," she said. She also exemplified Team Spirit.

I interviewed her supervisor. He said that there was a lot of construction going on at the hospital but Ril always found her way around it. He just shook his head with admiration. She didn't wander around going, "They should clean this mess up," "They" this or "They" that. She found a way to navigate it every day with a smile on her face.

Of course, how we adapt to change in today's world determines a lot regarding how far we go. Ril is an inspiration there as well. When technology advanced, having dark rooms became a thing of the past in most hospitals.

After being a dark room technician for 26 years, that job ended in 2002 as computers took over. Memorial Hospital wanted very much to keep Rill, so everyone worked to see where she could be best utilized. Rill was able to be redeployed in the Market Research Department on patient satisfaction survey mailings.

"I keep the inventory," she said happily. "I stuff the surveys. I love it! I'm extremely lucky I've had two jobs here and have loved both of them! I love life! I absolutely love it!!"

I have used video clips of Ril in motivational training sessions and her story has never ceased to impact people. I have people come up to me after my program and say how their attitude has been revitalized by her story. Her commitment to excellence in attitude, job pride, team spirit, and embracing change is one of the best I have ever seen.

There are cases where someone might say that it's hard to have a positive attitude or accomplish things in life when you come from a very tough background. That always makes me think of the feature I did on Dr. Amber Darey-Thomas. She had been raised in the Cabrini-Green housing project in Chicago, one of the roughest places in the U.S. I remember when I interviewed her for my television news feature story that I couldn't get over how much she smiled and how positive she had been and still was about life. "When I was seventeen, I set goals," she told me. When I met her she was in the early stages of her medical career as a doctor. "My goals were to graduate from college, go to

Med School, get married and have three kids. I did all of that. Well, I had two kids and not three, but I was not going to stop until I reached my goals!"

Dr. Darey-Thomas did something as a young person that is critical when it comes to positive attitude. She forged ahead. She didn't wait for opportunities. She sought them out. "The counselors at my school got so tired of me always asking if there was anything else for me to do to better myself that they sent me to D.C. to be a Page. That is what really turned me around. It showed me there was a life outside Chicago. I applied for and got medical scholarships and went after it (she is a family practice doctor today in Michigan). Don't ever give up. Dream it. Do it. Believe it! Nothing is unattainable as far as I am concerned. You may not have the support behind you but, if you strive, you can do it!"

The feature I was able to do on a man named Darrell left a lifelong impact on me as far as attitude. I actually observed him over four days when I was speaking at a Retreat. I noticed that despite physical challenges he was always upbeat and everyone gravitated towards him. When the Retreat was over, I sought him out to do a feature on him for my positive-news "Making a Difference" series on the news. I learned that, like Wayne, he had been born with cerebral palsy. In 1990, after a lifetime of work in Oregon, he had moved to northern Indiana with his wife of thirty-five years. But shortly after they moved, she died of cancer. That same year Darrell had a stroke, quadruple bypass surgery and, not long after that, he learned he had cancer. After finishing thirty-five chemo treatments, he had a bad fall and broke his hip. None of those major challenges would keep him down. Living at Greencroft Senior Housing, he dedicated himself to giving himself to others through gifts of love like volunteering to fold laundry on Wednesday's and the weekends. I remember when I interviewed him that it was difficult to understand him because his speech had been affected by his stroke, but I could hear him say, "I love to work with people and help people and do what I can."

He belonged to St. Mark's United Methodist Church. I went over there and interviewed one of their office folks and he said that Darrell had heard the news on the local access channel that their Church was having a fundraiser and he sold more tickets than any other person in the entire church.

"You can't keep him down," a fellow Church member told me. "I went to visit him in the hospital after he broke his hip, but he had already gone home. He will not let life's frailties keep him down. Our Church has grown because of him. He might have a headache (and he's gone through all kinds of things), but he still doesn't skip his volunteering or miss Sunday School or Church.

Everything is about our attitude. At the end of the feature, Darrell turned to me and said, "I don't know where I would be if it wasn't for the Lord. Have faith, courage, and hope." Despite all those medical challenges, his focus was on how grateful he was for a place to live and volunteer, a strong church, and his faith.

I have played video clips of their stories during hundreds of motivational seminars over the past ten years, and their stories never fail to inspire people to grow their positive attitudes.

Who is the most positive person in your life who is similar to the special people in this chapter?

____

____

____

____

— 7 —

Staying Positive Throughout the Day

BUILDING AND KEEPING a positive attitude is like building and keeping a good marriage or relationship. You have to work at it.

Any champion in life has certain fundamental things they do every day to reach peak performance. When it comes to positive attitude, it takes work and repetition to keep the darn thing. Some people are blessed with the "zippity-doo-dah" attitude no matter what and God bless them. Most of us, including myself and p-r-o-b-a-b-l-y YOU, have to work at it.

When organizations bring me in to work with their people on positive attitude, everyone gets a handout with an outline of a day. We go over what the heck to do throughout that WHOLE day to try to keep that darn positive attitude. Negativities swoop in and try to take it away! This chapter is dedicated to giving you lots of tools to not just make it through a day, but to thrive every day!

The start of the day is critical for setting the tone.

When I wake up, the first thing I do is literally slide out of the bed onto my knees and I thank God for the day. It isn't a very long prayer as I am usually desperate for coffee, but it certainly is important. The next thing I do is think of a book written by Greg Jaggers, entitled *When My Feet Hit the Floor.* As soon I get up and start walking for the coffee machine, I think positive thoughts. I have known Greg for years and he says that his thoughts during his first steps each day are:

- How do I get my day started?
- What do I do with the choices I have and how do I react to those choices?
- A belief with all my heart that those first steps are when our choices start and that it is yours and my option to either make or break each and every day.

Something you can do to really help build that positive attitude each day is to realize how grateful we all should be to be alive! The visualization I make is of something I have seen many times at Notre Dame Stadium, which is near where I live in South Bend, Indiana. I reported on Notre Dame for many years in my television-news days. Right after the games I remember walking towards the tunnel where the players exit to go to their locker room. I would always see young boys and girls hanging over the railing. Their hands were reaching out, hoping to catch a dirty, muddy sweatband or headband or anything with grass stains and the smell of football! I would always stop and watch as some of the players would take a sweatband off and toss it up to them. Those who caught one would clutch it with all their might, hold it out in front of themselves, and gawk at it with the expression of, "I got it!! I got it. I have it!!!"

That is how it is about each day. We HAVE it! No day is guaranteed. To build a positive attitude, it is important to focus on the blessing of the day that we have been given. Yes, I know many people have all sorts of challenges that will come throughout that day but, if you take time to appreciate the gift of it, then your positive attitude is fortified!

> Charlie, I have the good fortune of unbridled optimism fueled by the belief that life will always provide new opportunities if you are willing to look for them and act on them once they are presented. I understand the pain that comes from losses we all endure. I've had more of those types of losses than I would have ever wished, but my faith in the ability to recover is encouraged by beliefs instilled primarily by my parents and grandparents. They knew more than their fair share of trials and sorrows and loss, but also knew that the only way to survive a setback was to move forward with strength, courage and conviction. Faith is the willingness to believe that God will give you the ability to prevail over anything. It is our responsibility to keep after it until the day we're called to join Him and each and every soul that has preceded us. So until that day arrives, I will move forward and know that new fantastic memories are yet to be realized, but are waiting around the corner. I just have to turn that corner to catch up with them. Together we will prosper and thrive on this day!
>
> *– Jim Ritter, Insurance Agent*

Another important part of building a positive attitude is Quiet Time in the morning. No matter how busy I am or even if I am in another city with a 6:30 a.m. flight, I get up and allow enough time for...Quiet Time. This is a time for reflection, meditation, prayer and building an attitude foundation for the day. Does it mean that curve balls in life won't come your way? No! But it can help you deal with those as the day goes along.

> Charlie, I stay positive by practicing meditation daily. It helps me to get centered at the start of each day. When I'm in frustrating situations later on, I am able to access my "centered" feeling even in the midst of negativity. I can then BE the positive energy in the situation. Spending time in meditation each morning is as important to my daily routine as brushing my teeth. The silence is a very healing place to be, because it teaches you to BE present. Accessing the quiet, for me, is often as simple as sitting comfortably with my eyes closed and noticing my thought patterns, the pattern of my breath and hearing my own heart beat. Sometimes all I have is 5 minutes, but I'll take it! I also teach yoga for a living, but find time for my own daily practice. The yoga helps me meditate and the meditation helps me to practice yoga so it's win–win. The practice of going to that place of inner peace helps me in infinite ways when it comes to dealing with others, especially people who seem overly annoying, angry or negative. I simply send them my peace in the face of their quirks, rants and complaints. They may not know I'm doing this, but they can certainly feel my peaceful energy. I just look at them and see that "hey, this is person is acting at his or her capacity in this moment and they might have had some challenging

events leading up to this moment that is being acted out in front of me." I know that it's not personal. The practices of yoga and meditation have helped me to live in this feeling mode instead of a constant thinking mode, which ultimately helps me to love all people more. I almost always silently say "Namate" or "I love you" to everyone I encounter. Sounds kind of crazy offering up love to someone who is seemingly being a jerk but it's hard for my inner peace to be disturbed by someone I've silently told "I love you." By giving in this way, love has come back to me in ways I never thought possible.

– Julia Jonson Cohn, RYT

There is the story of a restaurant manager named Jerry. Each morning he wakes up and says to himself, "Jerry, you have two choices today. You can choose to be in a good mood or you can choose to be in a bad mood. I choose to be in a good mood. Each time something bad happens, I can choose to be a victim or I can choose to learn from it. I choose to learn from it. Every time someone comes to me complaining, I can choose to accept their complaining or I can point out the positive side of life. I choose the positive side of life." Life is all about choices. When you cut away all the junk, every situation is a choice. You choose how you react to situations. You choose how people will affect your mood. You choose to be in a good or bad mood. The bottom line is it's your choice how you live life.

Charlie, there are days when the sun shines bright and everything seems to naturally fall into place. There are other days when simply surviving seems like a signifi-

> cant accomplishment. Both extremes summon us to respond in kind: the first with awareness and gratitude, the second with courage and hope. To neglect the response, to mindlessly "escape" into trivial pursuits, is to live in the shallows and to squander the gift. I don't want to squander my gift. That is one reason why I must pray daily.
>
> *– Robert Kloska, Holy Cross College*

The gifted writer Max Lucado crafted these thoughts that I have printed out for my Quiet Time area:

> Today I will make a difference. I will begin by controlling my thoughts. A person is the product of his thoughts. I want to be happy and hopeful. Therefore, I will have thoughts that are happy and hopeful. I refuse to be victimized by my circumstances. I will not let petty inconveniences such as stoplights, long lines, and traffic jams be my masters. I will avoid negativism and gossip. Optimism will be my companion, and victory will be my hallmark. Today I will make a difference.
>
> I will be grateful for the twenty-four hours that are before me. Time is a precious commodity. I refuse to allow what little time I have to be contaminated by self-pity, anxiety, or boredom. I will face this day with the joy of a child and the courage of a giant. I will drink each minute as though it is my last. When tomorrow comes, today will be gone forever. While it is here, I will use it for loving and giving. Today I will make a difference.
>
> I will not let past failures haunt me. Even though my life is scarred with mistakes, I refuse to rummage through my trash heap of failures. I will admit them. I will correct them. I will press on. Victoriously. No failure is fatal. It's OK to stumble.... I will get up. It's OK to fail.... I will rise again. Today I will make a difference.
>
> *– Max Lucado*

I love it! The line about optimism will be my companion is solid gold. As you go through the day, visualize optimism as your actual companion. Another line that resonates is the one about refusing to rummage through trash heaps of failure. Copy and paste Lucado's writing. Put it next to your bed or where you have coffee in the morning. Use it as a tool to help build that positive attitude!

When I deliver the seminar on Attitude and everyone has that sheet of "Steps" for each day, I have a picture on it of a guy shaving and a lady putting makeup on in the morning.

That leads to the next step of thoughts during such things. In my case, when I shave I have positive thoughts each stroke of the ol' razor blade. Rather than stressing out with all the umpteen challenges that might be ahead, I think positive thoughts.

As you leave your home, take these two quotes:

> (1) "Don't have a great day...make it a great day!"
>
> – *Karen Phelps Moyer*

In other words, don't let a good day come to you. Grab it by the horns with your attitude of gratitude and make it a special day. Go on the offensive with what you say, how you respond to things, and how you celebrate the many blessings of the day.

> (2) "I told my kids early on that when you go out the door, choose happiness."
>
> – *Michael J. Fox*

Many of us know the story of Michael and his battle with Parkinson's. A positive attitude is about choice and, as a father, he has helped his children understand that they can choose happiness when they go out into the day.

Jack Harbaugh helped raise two sons who would one day face each other as opposing head coaches in the 2013 Super Bowl. Jim Harbaugh was head coach of the 49ers while John Harbaugh was head coach of the Ravens. When they were little, Jack would drive them to school. As they got out of the car he would say, "Okay, men, grab your lunch boxes and attack this day with an enthusiasm unknown to mankind!" Jack later shared this with Yahoo Sports!: "In this world, you can choose to be positive or you can choose to be negative. You can choose to see things through a set of eyes that sees good or you can choose to see things in life that aren't so good. At least every day, they were reminded to look at it through a positive set of eyes. Let the lens of your eyes be positive."

That's a great approach to use to go through your day! Tell yourself those things in the morning. If you have contacts or glasses, tell yourself you are putting on positive lenses.

There was a businessman who carried a card each day that read: "The way to happiness is to keep your heart free from hate, your mind from worry. Live simply, expect little, give much. Fill your life with love. Scatter sunshine. Forget self, think of others. Do as you would be done to."

As you go into your day, take this approach: "I get to…rather than I have to." Even if you have a blah job or a bunch of knuckleheads you will have to encounter throughout the day, hold onto that approach of you "get to" do those things. Think about those who would love to be healthy enough to go to a job. When you tell yourself you "get to" do something, there is more of a grateful approach. If you keep saying you "have to" do something, it comes across as some burden. The "get to" approach builds a positive in you, while the "have to" way brings on negative energies.

> All the years I have worked with Special Needs Kids have helped with a positive attitude as I am in each day. When one grabs your hand and tells you, you're my bff and I love you, it melts your heart. Your attitude changes in a second. I try to think about times like that when I am having a bad day.
>
> *– Roma Schroeder Bovenmyer*

As you leave your home and go out into…the world (dramatic drum roll, please), here is something to take with you that Bill Cosby told me years ago. I was in Chicago to interview him on the set of the show "Kids Say the Darndest Things." I found him to be very nice and filled with wisdom. He said, "Charlie, I don't know the secret of success, but I know the way to failure is trying to please everybody." Cosby has said that several times over the years, and I firmly believe that it is also a way to lose your positive attitude. Yes, you want to care about everything you do through the day but, if you think you are going to please everyone, good luck!

As you go through your day, be aware of the bounce in your step. Exude a positive energy as you move.

> I've learned to only worry about things I can control. I am also in a position that thousands of people would love to do as their profession, so feeling blessed to do what I do keeps things very positive.
>
> *– Darin Pritchett, sports talk radio host*

While Darin loves his job, many have jobs that are just that…jobs. I realize you may have knuckleheads at the workplace to deal with and that you may be understaffed, underappreciated, and overworked but early in the day…try to go in with the approach of you "get" to go to work rather than "having" to go to work. That entails thinking of so many people from impoverished countries or those who are in terrible health. Focus on the blessings you do have at work.

> Charlie, the way I look at it is that happiness is what we carry inside. Happiness is when you "Live Your Life Well," not from a materialistic aspect, but from a spiritual [aspect]. It's learning to put it in God's hands, to really put it in God's hands. Our human nature wants to be in charge, when the reality is, we really aren't in charge. If you try, and that's the important word, try, to live a Christ-like life, you will find an inner peace, kindness, joy and satisfaction no material thing can give. We all will fall short, but when we realize our weaknesses, we also learn it's OK. The ultimate goal is to strive to live a life knowing that someday, I will be in heaven with the Father. What greater goal to focus on is there? Through faith and the trust in knowing God has it handled, is what brings true happiness, inside and out.
>
> *– Tom Fisher*

The following is something else that I have printed out and read over once or twice a week during my quiet time or at some point in the day. Dr. Steve Maraboli, a speaker and author, wrote this and I think it rocks:

> Today, many will awaken with a fresh sense of inspiration. Why not you?
>
> Today, many will open their eyes to the beauty that surrounds them. Why not you?
>
> Today, many will choose to leave the ghost of yesterday behind and seize the immeasurable power of today. Why not you?
>
> Today, many will break through the barriers of the past by looking at the blessings of the present. Why not you?
>
> Today, for many the burden of self-doubt and insecurity will be lifted by the security and confidence of empowerment. Why not you?
>
> Today, many will rise above their believed limitations and make contact with their powerful innate strength. Why not you?
>
> Today, many will choose to live in such a manner that they will be a positive role model for their children. Why not you?
>
> Today, many will choose to free themselves from the personal imprisonment of their bad habits. Why not you?
>
> Today, many will choose to live free of conditions and rules governing their own happiness. Why not you?
>
> Today, many will find abundance in simplicity. Why not you?

> Today, many will be confronted by difficult moral choices and they will choose to do what is right instead of what is beneficial. Why not you?
>
> Today, many will decide to no longer sit back with a victim mentality, but to take charge of their lives and make positive changes. Why not you?
>
> Today, many will take the action necessary to make a difference. Why not you?
>
> Today, many will make the commitment to be a better mother, father, son, daughter, student, teacher, worker, boss, brother, sister, and so much more. Why not you?
>
> Today is a new day!
>
> Many will seize this day.
>
> Many will live it to the fullest.
>
> Why not you?"
>
> *– Dr. Steve Maraboli*

One way to lose your positive attitude is to let little annoying things pile up on you to where you start getting negative. You get to work and some of the clowns there agitate you to no end. In that case, try to be like the old broken-down mule! There once was this sad-looking and aging mule that fell down a shaft. The farmers came to rescue him but, realizing he was so old, they decided to leave him down there. They started shoveling in dirt so that the hole wouldn't be dangerous. The mule could have allowed himself to be buried but each time a load of dirt landed on his back he shook it off. Eventually it went down to his hooves and he rose up with it and walked out of the hole. Take that approach as you go through the day. When someone says or does something that chaps your butt and sours your attitude, visualize yourself as that mule and shake it off. Like the mule, you will rise up and stand above it!

> Charlie, here is part of a poem by Minnie Louise Haskins that I think of each day: "I said to the man at the gate of the year, 'Give me a light that I might out into the unknown.' He said to me, 'Go, place your hand in the hand of God. It is better than a light and safer than a known way.' "
>
> – *Herman Stenger*

Of course, remember the big three quotes from earlier in this book:

> "You can celebrate life or suffer life and it has absolutely nothing to do with your circumstances."
>
> – *Sandra Herron*

> "A positive attitude doesn't mean you can do anything but a positive attitude means you can do everything better than if you have a negative attitude."
>
> – *Zig Ziglar*

> "To *think* only of the *best,* to *work* only for the *best,* and to *expect* only the *best.*"
>
> – *The Optimist Creed*

> Charlie, as I go through a day I always thank God I was born in our wonderful country and understand things could be worse. Most of all...humor...I laugh easily at myself.
>
> – *Andy Gartee*

MaryEllen Tribby, founder and CEO of workingmomsonly.com, developed a success indicator that I think is of great value to you as you look at each day. She has a positive/negative counterpoint to things that includes these observations:

* Successful people compliment.
  Unsuccessful people criticize.
* Successful people have a sense of gratitude.
  Unsuccessful people have a sense of entitlement.
* Successful people forgive others.
  Unsuccessful people hold a grudge.
* Successful people accept responsibility for their failures.
  Unsuccessful people blame others for their failures.
* Successful people read everyday.
  Unsuccessful people watch TV everyday.
* Successful people keep a journal.
  Unsuccessful people say they keep a journal but don't.
* Successful people talk about ideas.
  Unsuccessful people talk about people.
* Successful people want others to succeed.
  Unsuccessful people secretly want others to fail.
* Successful people share information and data.
  Unsuccessful people horde information and data.
* Successful people keep a "to-be" list.
  Unsuccessful people don't know what they want to be.
* Successful people exude joy.
  Unsuccessful people exude anger.
* Successful people keep a "to-do/project" list.
  Unsuccessful people fly by the seat of their pants.
* Successful people set goals and develop life plans.
  Unsuccessful people never set goals.
* Successful people continuously learn.
  Unsuccessful people think they know it all.

* Successful people embrace change.
  Unsuccessful people fear change.
* Successful people give other people credit for their victories.
  Unsuccessful people take all the credit for their victories.
* Successful people operate from a transformational perspective.
  Unsuccessful people operate from a transactional perspective.

That boils down to a positive/negative perspective on all of those important points. Is there one area of Mary Ellen's list that you REALLY need to work on? If so, write it down here—and any others—and focus on them as you go through your day!

As we get into our day, someone or something will inevitably threaten to devour our positive attitude. By the midpoint of the day we can be like a boxer that has taken some body shots. Just like that boxer needs to get to his corner to rest and get encouragement from his corner man, we need to take a short attitude break. What I always do just before I eat lunch is take five long, deep breaths. On each breath I fill myself with positive thoughts. Granted, this may look odd if you are at a business lunch and the client awkwardly watches as you go into your little trance. In that case, I do it in the bathroom beforehand. Regardless, it helps. It also helps get you out of that mindset where you feel you have to run around like crazy all day. It slows you down.

Among those who submitted their positive attitude habits for this book, Anne and Dan shared how their faith helped them in adversity:

> "He may let you bend, but he will not let you break."
> – *Anne Nowak Borrelli*
>
> "If it's over your head, it's in God's hands."
> – *Dan Kiefer*

Many of us spend significant time driving. What do you do with that time? I realize not everyone is going to have a pack of motivational CDs in their car. Most folks probably pop on their local radio station. In many cases those radio hosts can be funny, informative and an important part of the day. I listen to inspirational CDs that I have and Christian talk radio. The average time spent in a car each year is 500 hours. That is around two college semesters. When I drive to speak in a neighboring state, I think of that as an opportunity to listen to positive CDs that will enhance my life and attitude.

> Working as a police officer for eight years really helped change my attitude towards life. It made me

> realize there is always someone out there who has it worse than I.
>
> – *Eric Haitsma*

Several years ago I made the decision to get rid of cable or satellite. It was one of the best things I did as far as impacting my positive attitude. As long as I can get my local channels to catch up on the weather, important news, and how my local sports teams are doing, then I am fine. I have all kinds of DVD documentaries and uplifting movies. An example of a DVD I have is *Soul Surfer*, the movie that is based on the true story of championship surfer Bethany Hamilton, who lost her left arm in a shark attack as a young person, yet came back to surf at top levels. My three kids and I saw it twice in the theater and my youngest and I have seen it multiple times at home. It is filled with the power of a positive attitude. For example, here are some quotes:

"I don't need easy. I just need possible." Bethany said this when she was training to learn how to surf again. Awesome quote!

"I wouldn't change a thing, because then I wouldn't be here talking to you. I can embrace more people now than I could with two arms." Bethany says this at the end of the movie as a swarm of media is around her after a competition. Her story had become international news and thousands of people from around the world wrote to her and were inspired by her comeback. Had she never been attacked by that shark, she wouldn't have had an impact on 99% of those people.

"For I know the plans I have for you, declares the LORD, plans for welfare and not for evil, to give you a future and a hope" (Jeremiah 29:11). Bethany's church youth pastor, played by Carrie Underwood in the movie, says this early in the film. God had a huge plan for Bethany's life and took that attack and turned it into something that helped so many people.

The extras on this DVD are powerful when it comes to positive attitude. They are among the best I have ever seen. There are several thirty-minute features on Bethany in real life and her comeback. There is one segment where she is being interviewed on a television show and the host says, "Bethany, if you are able to come back and..." Bethany interrupts him and says, "If? ... when."

Regarding positive books you can read at night or when you make the time, I asked my Facebook followers to share with me their favorite book on attitude. Here are some of the submissions:

The Game of Life and How to Play It by Florence Scovel Shinn

Outwitting the Devil by Napoleon Hill

Learned Optimism by Martin Seligman

PUSH by Chalene Johnson

The Road Less Traveled by Dr. M. Scott Peck

FiSH – a video based on the market in Seattle. Simple but amazing.

I'm Not Missing Anything by Brett Eastburn

A book I have read and re-read is *The Power of Positive Thinking* by Dr. Norman Vincent Peale. What I have done with that book and others like it is read them twice, then underline certain parts of the book. Next, I write out about three pages of notes in a notebook and over several days look over those notes once or twice each day. That way certain quotes or tools on how to stay positive soak into me, and I retain them.

At bedtime, one of the things I do is lay there and think about positive things that happened either that day or recently. I think about positive things my kids have been doing and positive relationships I have developed. I fill my mind with positive memories from recent days, and then I get excited about tomorrow. In my favorite book on attitude (*The Power of Positive Thinking*), Dr. Peale shares the story of a man who often reads the 23rd Psalm at bedtime. He says because of that he doesn't go to bed with an earful of trouble, but he goes to sleep with a mind full of peace.

> Charlie, I find that just trying to cultivate gratitude daily is important to me personally and in how I raise my kids. My girls and I end every day talking about our "favorite part of the day" right before prayers...and it's often not something I would expect them to say. And during that time, we also point out one or more things we are grateful for.
>
> *– Traci DuVal, local television anchor*

What are five action steps you are going to take from the ideas listed in this chapter?

____

____

____

____

____

____

____

____

____

____

— 8 —

The Positive Attitude of an Olympic Athlete

WHILE WE TRY TO STAY upbeat and positive with our attitudes, there are times in life when you get about as down as possible.

Olympic athlete Morgan Uceny slowly but surely got back up with her positive attitude after falling, literally, in the biggest race of her life. It was in the 2012 London Olympic Games. Raised on a farm in the small town of Plymouth, Indiana, Morgan worked hard to become an elite high school runner, a standout for Cornell, and as a professional she reached the #1 ranking the world in 2011 in the 1500 meter (just under a mile). She made the 2012 Olympic team and was entering the final lap of the 1500 final in London poised to either win or finish among the top runners. Known for her kick at the end, she was in position to medal. No American woman ever had earned any kind of medal in the 1500.

Back in her hometown, an overflow crowd packed her old high school to watch the race on a big screen.

Signs reading "Go Mo Go" were on every business. A street had been renamed in her honor by the mayor for that week. She was the first person ever from their area to make the Olympics! Many had said that Morgan had brought the entire community together. So many in the town had seen her growing up, running on country roads, and raising animals as a 4H-er.

Hard workers like Morgan deserved to shine at the Olympics. This is a person so humble that when back home from Cornell on college breaks, she would wash school buses as her mother, Brenda, used to be a school bus driver.

Then it happened. With a pack of runners behind her, Morgan was tripped. In a split second she was crashing to the track. Her chances of a gold or any medal were crushed. She had spent years of training and making sacrifices for that one moment. It was right there...

To watch it on NBC and see the pictures was about as gut-wrenching as anything I have experienced in awhile. After falling she slapped the track over and over in frustration. Then the tears flowed, right there in front of the crowd in the stadium and millions more watching on television. In what she would later call the most heartbreaking moment of her life, she cried and cried.

Later, she wrote to her thousands of followers on her Facebook fan page: "As soon as it happened I knew it was over and I couldn't control the emotions. I was able to see my family tonight, and I don't know what I would have done without them. They all shared my tears but also were

(courtesy *USA Today*)

the rocks of support that I needed. I feel like I'm in a dream, and that I will wake up tomorrow on August 10th to race the 1500m final over."

Earlier in this book I wrote about the Four Needs and one of them being Someone to Love. Morgan's family was critical in keeping her from diving into such a negative state. They couldn't help her get positive all of a sudden, but their love helped her make it minute to minute. One of the attitudes I talk about in the seminar "How to Build a Positive Attitude and KEEP the Darn Thing!!" is the encouraging attitude, and how it can lift people up. Over the next few days Morgan was about as down as a person could be, yet the encouragement came from around the world in the form of thousands of messages. Here are just a few:

> *My family too wept with you during that moment, Morgan, but we as everyone else and you know you made it there and tried—that's what counts. – Eric*

When it gets tough, and the darkness moves in to take you, fight your hardest, give it nothing less than your best and stay your course! Pray, read the Bible and trust God to make your path straight. Let him guide your feet to where you need to go. – Mattias

I saw a plaque today at a gift shop, "If you trip, make it part of your dance," and immediately thought of you. That one moment in time was so awful, but it does not define you, Morgan. You worked hard, made it to the OLYMPICS, made it to the final...all that is amazing! Your strength and perseverance define you. Your good-natured, fun-loving spirit is evident—those things define you. Your love of family defines you. Keep dancing, Morgan! – Lynne

You have no idea how much of a hero you are to the kids at Plymouth High School. Medal or no medal—you are a superior role model for countless kids that dream to be in your shoes. The entire town of Plymouth is beyond proud of you and we all shared in your tears. But, thank you for the amazing ride you took us all on and the joy you brought to everyone! You are amazing, you are an Olympic athlete, you are a role model, and you are a hero! – Bryan

Florence Griffith-Joyner said, "Success does not define a person but challenges do!" You are a very gifted athlete so hold your head high and keep your eye on the prize. Your time is coming! – Suzie

The support kept coming and the days moved along. Morgan left London for Italy where she had been doing some pre-Olympic training. Her lower back injured from the fall, she finally started doing some light jogging a few days later. It wasn't long before she wrote this:

"I've been on the verge of tears for almost an entire week...but today I was running along a bike path in Tus-

> cany with the sun shining on my face and I realized that it's time to get my head out of you know where. It will still take time to get the fall behind me, but it is not something that's going to define me. I've been riding my bike around town, stopping for an espresso here, a gelato there...and I realized: life is good if you let it be."
>
> – *Morgan Uceny, Saturday August 18, 2012*

Life is good if you let it be.

While Morgan came up short in her quest to medal at the Olympics, with what she wrote on August 18th she has motivated and inspired thousands and thousands of people around the world to take a grateful attitude through life. There will be crushing failures along the way, but never stop appreciating those moments when the sun splashes in your face.

She has brought her small hometown of Plymouth closer together than anything since their basketball team won the state championship in 1982. She has planted seeds of "you CAN reach your dreams" in more young children that we can possibly imagine.

It will be a long time before she ever gets over this, and she probably will never totally get past it, but the key is taking it one day at a time and building off the encouragement from others.

What has been a crushing defeat in your life—like what Morgan experienced at the Olympics?

____

____

____

____

____

After much heartbreak, what positives were you able to take from it?

What do you think about her perspective of "Life is good if you let it be?"

— 9 —

Balance Your Life

TO KEEP A POSITIVE ATTITUDE, it is vital to have a good grip on the balance between work and life. We all have so much going on that it is easy to get down on ourselves when we feel the whole work/life balance thing is out of whack. We feel guilty about certain things and it impacts our positive attitude. In many cases we put so many things on our life platter that we bring this stress on ourselves. There is an old saying that if you chase two rabbits you will lose them both.

In this chapter you will take away gems of wisdom from someone who has experienced the challenges of work/life balance for decades, Maureen McFadden. I emceed the Samaritan Counseling Center Awards Luncheon in my community, which is an annual event that recognizes local companies and organizations that are really good at work/life balance. Maureen is a longtime, successful news anchor at the NBC affiliate in South Bend where I live. Besides being a highly visible anchor, Maureen and her husband Jim are raising three boys. At the time of her talk, one had just graduated from Indiana University. Another is at Notre Dame. The third is in high school where he loves to play baseball!

Maureen told the audience that it was twenty years ago when her husband was hit by a drunk driver. This was before air bags. Though he is doing well now, that was quite the physical recovery challenge. Today Maureen is also very involved in caring for her elderly mother. She is in constant demand to appear at community events. As someone who was in TV News for almost a quarter of a century, I can tell you that her job as an anchor and reporter involves one challenge after another. So, when she speaks on work/life balance, it's like the old E.F. Hutton commercial—the audience listens.

After introducing her, I sat down and took these notes to share with you:

> Some days I am better at home. Other days I am better at work. I think that if my family knows I love them, and I make as many baseball games as possible, and look over homework, then I feel like I am doing my best.
>
> Young people today should understand the importance of balance. They often think they can do it all, and they cannot, and become hard on themselves. Here are things I do to help with balance in life.
>
> First, I pray. I am not putting religion on my sleeve in this talk and I don't care what your religion is. All I know is that prayer works for me. Prayer has taken me out of more jams than anything else in life. My dad was a [University of] Notre Dame man so my family grew up going to the Grotto. That is my "go-to" place. Prayer may not solve all my problems but it brings comfort.

Second, I have learned to just...say...no. It goes back to feeling we can accomplish everything. It took me years to realize I could not do it all. Maybe it's my Catholic guilt. When my husband was recovering from being hit by the drunk driver, and my kids were young, and I had work, a very wise woman—my mother—said it's okay to say no. If I needed to say no to going to read to school kids so that I could spend more time with my own family, then I said no to the school.

I used to freak out about having the perfect home and being the perfect wife and mother. Again, that very wise woman, my mother, said, "Maureen, when you die, do you want them to say she was a great housekeeper or a helluva woman?" If you come to my house today, you will see tenny shoes on the floor and an old-fashioned crock pot in the kitchen. The food in it is healthy and hot. I may not be a helluva woman yet, but I listened to my mother.

I'm not much into exercise. I know the younger people are these days. I do know it truly relieves stress. I go to the basement a few times a week and do the treadmill. However, if my mother needs help or if there is something with the kids, then I miss the exercise that day.

Another thing that helps me is humor. From the clowns I work with in the Newsroom to my kids and husband, I try to find humor in things. My husband and I went to see the new movie *The Three Stooges* and I thought it was hilarious. I had a good hard belly laugh for two hours!

We all have to work out what works best for us when it comes to work/life balance. None of us is getting out of this alive. Be kind to others. Do your best. Sometimes you strike out, but don't beat yourself up.

As our oldest son graduates from the Ernie Pyle School of Journalism at Indiana University, I am getting him a Dr. Seuss book, *Oh, the Places You Will Go!* It includes:

> You'll get mixed up, of course,
> as you already know.
> You'll get mixed up
> with many strange birds as you go.
> So be sure when you step.
> Step with care and great tact
> and remember that Life's
> a Great Balancing Act.
> Just never forget to be dexterous and deft.
> And never mix up your right foot with your left.
> *Oh, the places you'll go!* There is fun to be done!"
>
> *– Maureen McFadden, WNDU-TV,*
> *South Bend, Indiana*

I feel Maureen shares valuable insights and tools for us when it comes to work/life balance. Here are some of my thoughts about having work/life balance so that you keep that positive attitude:

You are human. There is only so much you can do. Do your best. Have a list of priorities for the day and take dead aim on accomplishing them. Curve balls will come which means they don't all get done. That's okay. If you did your best, you can be proud. When you are doing something, whether it is work or with your kids, make sure you are focused on it. It does no good to be thinking about how in the heck you are going to do the next thing, when you are doing something else.

Communicate. Let loved ones know that you are in a busy stretch at work and these are the reasons why it is so busy now. Explain that you truly want to be at their event, but in this case it won't be possible. By doing this, it prevents negativity from seeping in since you cannot be at a particular function.

One of the things that can really take a hit in work/life balance is exercise. No matter how wacky your schedule gets, do your best to prioritize a time to work out. If I have a normal day, I like to work out early in the morning at a local fitness center. On other days, I get it in later in the day. In some cases, I have to be creative. One of my daughters was with me at Concordia University in Wisconsin to watch my son run in a college cross-country meet. Because of driving and the events of the day, there would be no time to work out at a fitness center. We had an hour or so before he ran on the course, which was on a bluff overlooking Lake Michigan. The campus had a winding sidewalk down to the lake that included a bazillion steps. My daughter and I went over and I did the steps for 30 minutes. That was my workout for the day.

> "And on the seventh day God finished his work that he had done, and he rested on the seventh day from all his work that he had done. So God blessed the seventh day and made it holy, because on it God rested from all his work that he had done in creation."
>
> – *Genesis 2:2-3*

God took a break. So can you. For some of us, it is easy to get caught up in the go-go-go pace where you feel you have to be doing something all the time and that certain things won't make it unless you are doing something. Well, cemeteries are filled with irreplaceable people. I am not saying what you are doing in life isn't important, but make sure to regularly think about how you are doing when it comes to the balance of faith, family, work, exercise, and fun.

What is your biggest challenge when it comes to work/life balance?

What are two things you are going to do to improve the work/life balance challenges in your life?

— 10 —

The Most Positive Athlete Ever

AS A BROADCASTER who focused on positive news and peak performers, I had the opportunity to cover The Masters golf tournament during much of the 1990s. No doubt, the most positive man I ever interviewed there was Gary Player. Of the thousands of people I have interviewed about attitude, he ranks in the Top Five as far as truly showing what an incredible impact a positive attitude and a commitment to fitness can do for individuals and organizations.

Player was one of the greatest ever to play golf, winning The Masters three times as well as the U.S. Open, the British Open, and the PGA Championship. When he played The Masters for the final time in 2009, he received two days of standing ovations from the fans at the famed Augusta National Golf Course. I am convinced the love he received was as much for his incredible positive attitude and his unwavering belief that age is just a number, as it was for his success winning golf championships.

When I interviewed Player in April of 1998, he was 62. I knew of him, but had never met him. As I stood beside him near the Champions Locker Room, I sincerely felt the positive energy come from him. I asked him about age.

"One day a man of 60 will win Augusta," Player told me. "Of course, in today's modern era, one cannot adjust his mind to say that will happen. If you speak to gerontologists, people will be living to 130 years of age with diet, exercise and mindset. That's going to happen. So a man of 60 one day will be the equivalent of a man of 30 today. That's a medical fact."

As he spoke to me, his caddy was munching on an apple. The man's outlook rubs off on those close to him!

He walked the Talk that particular week in 1998. He went on to make "the Cut" at age 62, becoming the oldest man ever to play into the weekend at The Masters. At the time of the writing of this book, Player is past his mid-70s and still does 1000 sit-ups each day. As I always say, success leaves footprints. What are his favorite books and his approach to life?

His three favorite books are: *The China Study* (nutrition), *The Power of Positive Thinking* (Norman Vincent Peale), The Holy Bible.

Just a few years ago, he told *BBC Learning English* that his role models were Sir Winston Churchill, former South African President, Nelson Mandela, and Mother Teresa of Calcutta. "What all these people have in common is that each one of them was or is a very positive person, looking to overcome adversity rather than succumbing to it," he told BBC.

"Every morning when I wake up, I make a conscious decision to have a good day, to find the good in people and to have a positive impact on everyone that I come into contact with. This attitude has helped me throughout my golfing career, where I was perhaps not the most talented, or the biggest or the strongest, but I certainly had the determination to succeed.

> Now that I am in my 70s, there is no reason to change this way of thinking. Perhaps my days of winning major championships are over, but making a difference in people's lives is not. If more world leaders could find a way to lead their people this way, perhaps we would have fewer conflicts around the globe. Now wouldn't that be wonderful?
>
> – *Gary Player*

Gary Player attributes his success in life to these ten commandments he follows:

(1) Change is the price of survival.
(2) Everything in business is negotiable, except quality.
(3) A promise made is a debt incurred.
(4) For all we take in life we must pay.
(5) Persistence and common sense are more important than intelligence.
(6) The fox fears not the person who boasts by night but the person who rises early in the morning.
(7) Accept the advice of the person who loves you, though you like it not at present.

(8) Trust instinct to the end, though you cannot render any reason.

(9) The heights of great people reached and kept were not attained by sudden flight, but that while their companions slept were toiling upward in the night.

(10) There is no substitute for personal contact.

What are two things from Gary Player's approach to attitude that you can apply to your life?

— 11 —

Helpful Tools to Manage Your Time

ONE OF THE THINGS that can get us down on ourselves and take away our darn positive attitude is when we don't manage our time better. It gnaws at you and you become more negative. The more organized you are, the more positive you can be about life. Having things more under control and feeling like you are prioritizing things correctly leads to a good, calm feeling.

Coach Mandy Green has learned a lot about organization in her life, and has helpful insights here for you. I spoke at a conference in Boston where she was one of the presenters. After my presentation, I sat in the back of the room and took in depth notes on her talk on Time Management. Mandy is the head coach of the women's soccer team at the University of South Dakota. At the time of her presentation, over the span of two years, Mandy had married her husband Josh, had a son, moved with her family multiple times, and taken over a college sports team that had been struggling.

She has since built a championship foundation with

her team (seventeen of her players were Academic All-Conference on one of her most recent teams) at work, and spent the kind of quality time with her husband and son that she was determined to do. However, she knew to do these things she had to get better at organization. She studied the subject relentlessly by reading numerous books and articles. When she made her presentation, she said these were things that worked for her and that could be of help to others.

Her first point was that you should *"Own your Agenda"* each day and that taking back your agenda starts with your mindset.

"The first hour sets the tone for the day," said Mandy. "You need that positive mental diet from the start. Who gets up and watches the morning news? I did until I read the book *Compound Effect* which said, with kids in the house, would you let a stranger in to talk about destruction, murder and other negative things? I read that and said, 'No way am I having the morning news on again!' "

Mandy also brought up an interesting point about hydration. "When you wake up, your body has been in the desert for eight hours," she said, referring to not having water to drink while sleeping. "I drink a liter of water early on. I feel the caffeine you can drink just sucks the moisture, nutrients and energy out of you like a sponge."

Like many of us, Mandy spends a good bit of time in her office. That can mean starting the day by opening email.

"Before I open my inbox, I review my Vision for what I want to accomplish professionally," said Mandy.

"Use your Vision as your filter. People often do what is most urgent rather than what is most strategic. As far as emails, they can be addictive and you find yourself doing what your inbox tells you rather than what you tell yourself. I made a challenge when I started this to get my inbox down to 50 emails by that Friday. It was tough but I did it. And when it comes to computer use, browsing is the death of productivity."

Mandy follows two guidelines when starting her day: (1) Who do I need to reach out to? (2) Who am I waiting on?

She encourages people to look more seriously at lists and priorities.

"Have a master to-do list at the beginning of the month," she said. Have a daily to-do list with "A" next to your high priority things, "B" next to those not quite as high, and "C" on the next highest. "Parkinson's Law says, 'Work expands to fill the time allotted for it.' If you have two hours of work to do and an entire day in which to do it, the work will tend to expand gradually, and will take you all day long to complete the two hours of work. If you only have an hour, you'll work much more quickly and efficiently so as to complete it in that one hour. Use this law by setting deadlines for yourself that force you to complete the task far sooner.

"I have become more serious about time blocking," she said. "My husband is my assistant coach in soccer. He knows when my door is closed that it is time-block time and that if he comes in he will get that look that only women can give."

As I took notes on her presentation, I put a star by

several things, including this gem: "Go to work like you are going on vacation tomorrow," she said. "How productive are you when you are about to go on vacation? Very much, huh? Try that pace on a normal day and you'll be surprised by how much you accomplish."

I have known Mandy for several years and can tell you she is an intense, "on fire" person. One of the things she has learned to do is step back at times.

"Take a break every forty-five or sixty minutes," she said, "even if it is to go to the bathroom, which you will be doing a lot if you listen to my advice on drinking more water!! A short break allows the mind to get away and some of your best ideas may come from a short walk or even in the bathroom. How many times have you come up with great ideas while jogging! Try to take a vacation every ninety days. You will come back refreshed."

Mandy was very serious when she made the choice to become more organized.

"I did the Time Tracking," she said. "It's interesting. It's a pain! Ideally, you can do it for three weeks. Want to know where your money is going? I stopped spending money because I didn't want to have to pull out that note pad!!"

When it comes to meetings, how many times have you been in them when they start on task and then ramble and then go on and on...?

"First," said Mandy, "have a purpose and stick only to that purpose. Second, your meeting should start on time. Third, your meeting should end on time. To sum up, if you say you are going to have a meeting from 11:30 to 12:00 to discuss a certain topic, you better start your meeting at 11:30, it better be about the topic for the day and nothing else, and it better be over by 12:00."

As she said that, it reminded me of being at another conference when speaker Dan Tudor said that, to keep meetings on task, everyone should stand during the entire meeting. I bet that would cut those 45-minute meetings to 17 minutes!

"The requirement for every great achievement," she said, "is presence and focus. Multi-tasking is the antithesis of productivity. It has been estimated that the tendency to start and stop a task, to pick it up, put it down and come back to it can increase the time necessary to complete the task by as much as 500%. When you are multi-tasking, your energy and focus are all over the place and you are just half-assing things. This is why coaches feel like they are not productive enough and they feel guilty about how much they have achieved in the office because they know that they are only giving 20-40% of themselves to anything because they are distracted. They know that all of these other things are going on. The IQ of people who juggle email and work simultaneously falls by 10 points. Maximum performance is possible only when you concentrate single-mindedly on the task—the most important task—and you stay at it until it is 100 percent complete....

"The four basics are sleep, water, exercise, diet," she said. "I know that this seems basic and that I am preaching to the choir, but this is fundamental to stamina and strength. Most coaches are not sleeping and hydrating enough. Peak and optimal performance comes from people who are rested and consistently get 7-9 hours of sleep a night. They have equated the fact that, if you don't get sleep for a few nights, you are legally drunk. Daniel Amen, in his book *Use Your Brain to Change Your Age*, says that, if you are not getting a lot of sleep, it means that you are not going to be getting as much blood flow to your brain. Lack of blood flow to major organs causes premature aging of the organ."

Continually ask yourself, "What is the most valuable use of my time, right now?" And whatever it is, work on that. Your ability to discipline yourself to work on those few tasks that can make the greatest difference in your life is the key quality that makes everything else possible for you.

I hope Mandy's insights can help you with life organization so that you can keep your fire stoked as brightly as possible!

What is your biggest challenge with time management?

____
____
____
____
____
____
____
____

Write down what you are going to do about it so that you can feel more positive about how you are spending the time in your day.

—12—

Mel Tillis Stays Positive!

I HAVE HAD THE OPPORTUNITY to host many group travel trips for Edgerton's Travel over the years, including several to Branson, Missouri. On one such trip, Mel Tillis (famous for stuttering when he speaks but not when he sings) was performing. Between songs he looked out at the audience and shared this story:

"Wuh…wuh…wuh…when…I...I was a little kuh…kuh…kid my mother was worried about my s-s-s-stuttering so sh…sh…she held me back a grade in school. It didn't wuh…wuh…work but that's oh...oh…oh…okay because…I've been able to make a helluva living because of it!!"

The audience roared. Mel had a point. What appeared to be a severe liability as a child, a serious stuttering issue, turned out to be the major reason he is a famous singer and entertainer today. You could make the argument that, if Mel Tillis didn't stutter, he wouldn't really stand out from the rest of the pack!

— 13 —

The Role of Exercise and Nutrition

LET'S CUT TO THE CHASE when it comes to how exercise helps your positive attitude. Elle, played by Reese Witherspoon in the movie *Legally Blonde* (MGM 2001), summed it up best: "Exercise produces endorphins. Endorphins make you happy!" There!

Seriously, as you can see in the picture of me in this book, I care about fitness. This has made a tremendous impact on my positive attitude. Weatherman Al Roker has a saying that I really like: "Nothing tastes as good as skinny feels." Whether we are able to reach skinny or not, Al is right because when you are in good shape and eating well you have a constant good feeling.

There is a crying need for better fitness and nutrition in the United States and around the world. As a speaker and writer I feel a responsibility to motivate others to focus more on fitness. Exercise and eating well play a huge role in why I am positive. I am not here to get you to try to look like someone on the cover of *Men's Health* or *Shape* magazine, but I do want to challenge you. If you are a leader in any capacity, then please look at it as your responsibility to be in decent to good shape. Our school kids are fighting obesity like never before in our nation's history. If you are a principal or teacher, don't you think they are looking to you for fitness motivation? If you are a company leader, look at it as part of your job to maintain a level of fitness that will be a good example to those in your office. As a parent you play a large role in what your kids will do for exercise and diet for the rest of their lives. If you need an incentive to exercise, tell yourself that it is going to help you live longer for those you love, whether you have children or grandkids or nieces and nephews.

I am past fifty years old and can tell you that exercise and eating right are the reasons I am in this shape. I wanted to share with you the key things that I do.

EXERCISE:

The first thing I do is make it a priority to fit exercise in somewhere just about every day. My schedule is different all the time. If home, I try to work out early in the morning at the place I go locally, the ICE Athletic Center (ICE stands for I Can Excel). If I am traveling, I use whatever the hotel has to offer and, if they don't have much, I do pushups, sit-ups and cardio boxing in my room (or outside if the weather is good). I do little things like taking the steps instead of the escalator. If I am in a big airport that has the option of steps or escalator, I will take the steps two at a time. There are times I am the only one doing it.

I don't go into the fitness center or gym with the burden of knowing I have to do certain machines or exercise a certain amount of time. I see people walking around with clipboards that have all these sets of ten that they have to do and 'have' is the key word. They often look like they are in a prison, trudging around from machine to machine. If it is a day where I want to focus on chest and arms, I will have a variety of machines from which to choose. I may look at one and say, "Okay, you!" I will do a number of reps. It could be eight. It could be thirteen. I just do them and do them right. That way I am not going, "seven more...." You have to have a personal responsibility with this approach, but it works for me. The main thing is that I stay on myself to be doing *something* and not just standing around being Mr. Social.

I do group classes. I find there is a bond in group classes where you can feed off the energy of those around you. Everyone is working hard and that can inspire you and keep you going. At first I was reluctant to try group classes, so what I did was drag my 19-year-old (at the time) son with me when he was home from college during break. If you find yourself hesitant to go, do your best to get a friend or relative. I know the first time you do a group class is scary because everyone else has been there a bunch and knows the routine. Just get in there and take it step by step, and before long you will be having a very positive experience. Hey, I have done Zumba Hip Hop! If I can do that class, then you can do anything! I have done everything from Zumba

Hip Hop to Body Pump to Insane Abs to Turbo Kick and on and on.

Swimming: When I have access to a pool, I have this crazy-looking, dog-paddling routine that is really good for cardio. I turn around and around in the water as I dog paddle. I then do these breast stroke-looking things for a few laps. I draw a few stares, but it works.

> Charlie, as far as exercise I like Barre, Zumba, dance of any kind with great music. I also love to walk in the woods and believe in "earthing"...touching trees, walking in sand, and barefoot to get the earth energy.
>
> – *Wendy Wolf Bradford, Pharmacist*

I have a personal trainer, Cindy Wagner, that I work with on a regular basis. I do not need to set up sessions with Cindy so that I will come to the fitness center. I am self-motivated. However, I think many people do need that kick in the rear that comes with knowing a trainer will keep them accountable in sessions. I work with Cindy because she shows me all kinds of different exercises that I work into my routines.

She is a former pro beach volleyball player, equestrian polo player/trainer, and is a Latin ballroom-dancing competitor. She has 18 years experience as an NASM, ISSA-Certified Personal Trainer. One of the things she did for personal motivation earlier in her life was go for "her vein!" I want to share that story in hopes it can motivate you as well to reach a certain physical fitness goal that is realistic for you!

One day I was lifting weights. Close to me were these two big, muscular guys with their chests all puffed. They seemed to be in their late twenties. We all looked up on the TV that was above us as the local NBC affiliate was airing a taped segment where a TV Host was interviewing Cindy about fitness. The two strappin' guys watched it for a minute, and then I overheard their conversation:

> STRONG GUY ONE: *"Hey, that's the chick that is a trainer here!"*
>
> STRONG GUY TWO: *"Yeah, she is in shape, and she has got to be like 40 or something!"*
>
> STRONG GUY ONE: *"I know, dude. You know... that chick...she's got a vein!!"*
>
> STRONG GUY TWO: *"That is the ultimate, man! A chick with a vein!"*

I chuckled to myself as, for one, I had not heard someone called a "chick" in forever; and, two, there is a motivational lesson in "the vein." Those two serious lifters were totally sincere in their admiration for Cindy because she had worked out so hard over the years that a vein clearly showed on her muscular and toned arms. Whether you are into serious fitness or not, we all should have a goal out there like "the vein." One thing I have learned about Cindy is that she has "the fire within" and is passionate about helping others in fitness. Cindy truly believes she has been put on this earth to help people, which led her to personal training.

"I love changing people's lives, not just physically but mentally as well," she told me. That is her fire! The "Stoke" messages are about the importance of individuals and organizations finding their fire, and keeping it stoked with a constant pursuit of excellence!

One day after a training session, I sat down with Cindy in the lobby of I.C.E. and asked her to share a little of her story:

"Charlie, it all started in high school when I saw Rachel McLish (female bodybuilding champion). I wanted that toned physique with muscle. She had a vein in her arm that I could see, and I thought that was so cool. It motivated me! I started working out and reading how to achieve muscle, and it got to where I was in the gym six days a week for three hours a day. Others were going out. I would be in the gym. People knew that I had a goal to have that vein. Then, in college, there was a contest one time where whoever came back from summer break in the fittest shape would win $500. I said 'I'm winning it!' I trained all summer long and won the prize."

Cindy kept training, developed strong nutrition habits, and eventually got "the vein."

"At my 20-year high school reunion, my friends were saying, 'You got your vein!' "

Getting "a vein" in life is not easy. So many people want to take shortcuts, or don't realize that anything worthwhile will take work, dedication, and sacrifice.

> Charlie, people have to understand that you have to sacrifice for a length of time. Everyone wants it in an instant, like a pill.
>
> – *Cindy Wagner*

If you would like to have Cindy work with you as a personal trainer, you can reach her at: cinsferrari@yahoo.com.

So, what will be your "vein" as far as physical fitness goals? Be realistic. Cindy is a professional. But take a minute here to write down what your vein will be and what you will do to achieve it.

> I believe in NATURAL exercise. I have a triple-wide lot and a driveway, totaling a half-acre. I'm 65 and do the mowing myself. In the winter I shovel the snow from my walks and driveway. When I get old, I might slow down a tad, maybe.
>
> *– Bob Sheler*

Okay, back to my approach to fitness.

I listen to my body. I try not to push it too far, especially since I am in my 50s. I am not one of those macho guys in the weight room asking someone to "spot" me while I try to bench-press 350 pounds. I could care less about being able to lift massive weights. There was this one time when I was doing a class and, all of a sudden, we had these big tractor tires to lift. That caught me off guard and I bent over the wrong way and wrenched my lower back. That was dumb on my part. At my age and height (six-foot-five), I should have listened to my body and not bent over like I did to try to lift up that tire.

> I go to the B-Fit here in the small town I live in. I have discovered the wonderful world of Kick Boxing! I went to Dick's Sporting Goods and bought UFC gloves and I do my own workout with the bag. Going through a breakup at Christmas left me very negative and, of course, a tad angry. Punching that bag every night helped me control my feelings and I got a great workout in the process.
>
> – *Cindy DeMaso Beals*

The cardio machine I swear by is the Stepmill. It is basically a big ol' black machine where you step and step and step and step. After warming up, I will set it to level sixteen and go hard for a minute or so and then hit stop and rest for thirty seconds or so. When the clock gets back down to a few seconds, I hit start again and go for a minute or so. I do this for awhile and sweat like crazy. I can feel the calories pouring out of me. Like with weights, I don't have the approach of having to go twenty minutes. I think that makes it too much like a chore.

> I do daily circuit training...the "Insanity" workout with Shaun T. It boosts metabolism, increases energy, and helps to speed up healing when sickness is trying to knock you down and take you out. It is great for your skin and complexion and helps you lose weight or maintain. It builds muscle tone (shall I go on...ah-haah?). LOVE IT!
>
> – *Kimberly Ann Bonds*

I also get on the treadmill and set it to such angles as 5.0, 7.5, 10.0, 12.5 and then 15 with speeds ranging from 4.5 to 5.5. I go for about 50 to 70 hard seconds then straddle the sides and rest while sipping some water. Because of the wear and tear on my knees I don't run outside that much anymore. My body has told me that, at my age and size and weight (225 pounds to go with that 6'5" frame), there are more negatives than positives to running outside. I try to run a few 5Ks and 10Ks, but my training for them mainly comes from the machines. There is a local park with some big hills that I go to several times in the summer. I start at the bottom of the big hill and run to the top. I rest briefly, walk back down, and do it again. I jump rope every few days to throw something new into the routine. I like to box against the bags.

> I dance to music that I love and focus on that positive energy that is flowing through the music and my veins. It brings things into perspective and releases negative energies and will often snap me into a better frame of mind. I listen to Third Day, Christian rock or old R&B, blues music. I roller blade too and listen to music. I just have to have music and movement of some kind a few times a week. I kayak in the summer also. I think we all have stresses in life. We sometimes don't spend enough time with ourselves, so I try to find activities that allow me to free my mind. Often I am just listening and observing and taking it all in when that feeling alive spirit that we all have comes back to me. It's like the bell for recess sounds off and I go. I call it Sana Land. It's like that when I work too, so it's just a different type of focus and one that I really enjoy."
>
> – *Sana Kelly Powers*

NUTRITION:

Positive or negative. That's usually the case with what you eat. What I do is have an imaginary gate guard at my mouth. Before anything goes in, that gate guard comes out of his little booth and checks it out. If it is negative food, he sends it back. If it is positive, he lets it in. Another technique I have used over the years is breaking up with certain food. I will tell the food something like this: "You know, you have been fun but this just isn't working out. I am going to have to break up with you. Now, before you get all upset, you have to realize that there are plenty of other people out there who will be glad to have you. Don't get all sad on me."

For breakfast I usually have a healthy cereal with bananas, blueberries and almonds. I will follow that up with a Greek yogurt or a couple of hard-boiled eggs. As the day goes on I eat four to five mini meals. Rarely do I have a big meal. I also am methodical. I mentioned Al Roker earlier in this chapter. He once was asked about "Today Show" host Matt Lauer being in such great shape. Roker said that Lauer works out very hard at the gym and eats the same thing for breakfast and lunch every day. THAT is a key. It may not be exciting to folks, but it can work. I read that when she was on the show "Friends," Jennifer Aniston had the same salad on set every day. When Tiger Woods got in such great shape, I read that he had a steady dose of grilled chicken breasts and broccoli. Early in the week I grill a bunch of chicken breasts on my George Foreman grill and have those at lunch. To give them some extra taste I put brown mustard on my plate. I eat periodically during the day. I mix in some veggies from my local Farmer's Market, and drink lots of water throughout the day. I keep apples in my car to munch on.

> You want to change a person's attitude? Change what they eat. It's amazing!! Yep, exercise and run and lift, and then eat like crap!?! You cannot exercise your way out of poor nutrition. People just waste their money.
>
> – *Edward Kramer*

A nutritionist once did a program at my church and suggested that, when shopping at the grocery store, you should do most of your shopping on the perimeter of the store. That's where most of the natural healthy food is located. The processed bad stuff is usually within those perimeters. I try to do most of my shopping as he says, on the outside. I also go to my local Farmer's Market at least once a week and get all kinds of good healthy foods. What I have found, and this is no staggering revelation, is that you can work out and do all kinds of cardio but, if you are not eating wisely, then you are not going to get that fit or cut look, especially when it comes to abs. It really comes down to discipline.

When I swing by a Starbucks or something, I get a big green tea. I drink a lot of water throughout the day. I have cut out desserts except for when I host an Edgerton's group travel trip. As far as products, I am a believer in Advocare. I like the integrity of the company and the quality people who use their products—like quarterback Drew Brees.

A big reason why I was able to get into peak shape

was that I quit drinking alcohol. Once I did that, I became "cut" in a matter of weeks. I was doing all that working out and eating pretty well, but the empty calories of the alcohol was keeping me soft in the mid-section. Once I stopped hitting the sauce, I was amazed how quickly my body became hard and toned—in my early 50s! If you are going to reach any major goal in life, there will have to be sacrifice. With me, it was giving up the alcohol and I have not regretted it since.

Getting in good shape is going to require all of us to give up some things. Jeff Rea is the former mayor of Mishawaka, Indiana, and currently the President/CEO of the Chamber of Commerce of St. Joseph County. I see Jeff several times a year. When I saw him at an annual Day of Prayer event in my community a few years ago, I just about fell over backwards. "Man, you are in GREAT shape!" I blurted out. I hardly recognized him. Mayor Jeff had stoked the fire within to make a lifetime change in his fitness. Here is his amazing story than can kindle the flames of fitness dedication within you!

Mayor Rea was 247 pounds in January of 2007. By August of that same year, he was down to 167 pounds. He has stayed around that weight ever since. I called him up because I wanted to know how he did it and how he keeps the weight off. Here is what he told me:

> Charlie, I brought a Wellness person in to speak to our team at City Hall when I was mayor of Mishawaka. She did weight and body-fat testing and talked to us. Based on her charts, she told me I would classify as "obese." I was like, "Come

on..." Hearing that, and having a history of heart trouble in my family, got me going.

That stoked the fire within him!

Charlie, I didn't do a fancy diet. Instead, I set my mind to eat better and smarter. My schedule as Mayor had me grabbing a Coke here, a candy bar there. I cut out soft drinks. I had been having seven or eight a day—that's 180 calories each and all the sugar. I switched cold turkey to water. That was tough, and I got headaches. Now I use Crystal Light flavor packs in water. I started eating wheat bread instead of white. Eating out, I would eat half the portions and take the other half back for lunch the next day. I tried to focus on what I was eating late at night. I cut out the bag of chips at 9 at night. They say if you can repeat a pattern 12 weeks, it is ingrained in you. That's what happened to me. You train your stomach. I had a chili-cheese dog at the golf course the other day. My stomach said, "Jeff, we don't eat those anymore."

Charlie, I think diets take off weight real fast, but people put it back on fast. I lost 75 pounds over this time by setting a simple but powerful goal—to weigh less than the week before. That really works. During the first 52 weeks, I lost 50 pounds. Sometimes it was just a few ounces, sometimes a pound.

When I started all of this, I started walking for half an hour a day. That led to riding my bike and then I started running. I had never run before. Now, I run five miles every other day. I ran the Sunburst 5K [which finishes at historic Notre Dame

> Stadium] in 24 minutes, which is amazing to me. I have been doing the little stuff—walking to work and taking the stairs instead of the elevator.
>
> My doctor has been on me for years about my family history of heart troubles. I didn't want my first heart attack to be the thing to get me in better shape. The power of encouragement has really helped me. Even though some people think I have been battling an illness or had gastric bypass, the ones who know I did this through smart eating and exercise are so encouraging. I was walking to work one day back when I was mayor and a lady watering her flowers said, "You look great, Jeff! Keep it up!" As I sat at my desk, I kept thinking of what she said.
>
> I have gone through two major wardrobe changes. I did not save any of my "fat" clothes. They are all gone. I don't plan on going back to where I was.

When Jeff went out for his first run, he couldn't run around the block. Slowly but surely, through diet and exercise, he got in shape. Just over two years after he started all of this, he ran the prestigious Indianapolis Half-Marathon. Then, on his 40th birthday, he ran the Mayor's Marathon in Anchorage, Alaska.

"Telling people that I was going to go to Alaska to run a marathon kept me motivated to keep going," he said. "The last thing I wanted to do was come back and say that I didn't make it or didn't do it. I would have loved to take the people of Mishawaka along with me—they were such an encouragement."

He says he struggled a little between miles 22 and 24, but otherwise felt good. Rea finished the race in just under four hours and twenty minutes. Jeff said he had two goals—to finish the race and to do it in under four-and-a-half hours.

Regarding fitness, I have done a number of motivational seminars for Forest River Recreational Vehicles over the last decade. Floyd Miller, the operations manager of one of their plants, would bring me in so that I could work with his people on peak performance and positive attitude.

I have always felt that a leader who emphasizes physical fitness helps set a tremendous example for his people. Floyd has always been committed to being in shape, and it has helped him a great deal. At age 60, he was in Paris where he ran the Marathon de Paris. He finished it in three hours and 56 minutes, which is Boston Marathon-qualifying time for his age range. He had set a goal—to run marathons on all seven continents—and he reached that goal! "I'm just so driven by the beauty of this world," Floyd told me.

Floyd has been a leader for over three decades. He worked his way up through the ranks. Being fit has helped him tremendously. "You feel so much better about yourself," he said. "No matter what you do, exercise washes away the stress inside. I think of things when I exercise. It clears your head, makes you more alert!"

"Positive attitude is everything," he said. "I have always told my people to hang around positive people. It's amazing how fast negative people can drag an organization down. I've had to literally fire people because they were so destructive with their attitude."

The great majority of his workers have been positive, team-oriented people over the years. I did want to know how he dealt with the inevitable negative workers that we always have (...or *maybe* have been ourselves at one point...or two!).

"We normally pull the negative-attitude people aside and talk to them verbally," he said. "If that doesn't work, then write them up. But when you talk to them face to face and just say, 'What's going on?' you'd be surprised how many times you can help them turn it around. Many times it's something from their home, and you have to understand that. Many times I have helped them to see a doctor. I will move them to a more upbeat department if I can. Most of the time you can stop it, but the people who are *mad at the world,* you can't really help. As time goes on today, with road rage and all the anger built up, dealing with attitude becomes more important. The goal is to strive for the attitude of gratitude, to somehow put out a smile so that others say, 'I wish I had that.' "

Floyd chuckled when recalling how he has dealt with *"very talented* but *bad attitude"* workers. "Two or three times, because they had so many good things to offer, I made them the group leader! Sometimes they would pick up the ball. That got them going! I made a mistake doing that once, though. Bad mistake. The man was smart, but the attitude was bad."

He added: "In my Christian life, as a leader I've treated people fair. I've been up front, been an honest person. That makes for a relationship where people trust you as a leader."

Back to fitness and challenging yourself, Floyd told

me that of all the things he has done as far as marathons, NOTHING compares to the Antarctica Marathon! Floyd was one of 188 people from 14 countries to run the unbelievable course a few years back. Getting there was as much of a challenge as the actual run.

In Ushuaia, the southernmost town of Argentina, his group boarded a Russian ship called the *Akademik Loffe*, which was formerly used for spy operations. The group spent another 2½ days crossing the Drake Passage, which is considered the roughest water passage in the world. It is the place where not only are there high and strong winds that blow most of the time, but also the "Circumpolar Current" is squeezed through its narrowest gap. This is a westerly flowing current that flows around Antarctica powered by Antarctic winds. It flows at the rate of around 140 million cubic meters of water per second, or the equivalent of 5000 Amazon rivers.

Once he got there, Floyd found that their group was about all that was there.

"Even though there are no residents on this island," Floyd told me, "there are four scientific base camps with people manning these camps. They come from Chile, Argentina, Russia and China. These scientists are very cautious about who is allowed to come to this location. Let's just say this is political. Each one of these countries must give their approval and then preparations are made by our U.S. Embassy. In fact, approval was not granted until one week before the scheduled marathon! It had rained for two days straight before we got there so, in many areas of the race, we had mud up to our ankles. Part of our course was on rocks, glacier and many hills. I must say this was the worst terrain I have ever experienced. It felt like being on another planet.

"I read a book called *The Coolest Race on Earth*," said Floyd. "In there it talked about possible high winds, which we experienced on our trip home where we had up to 25-foot waves. In my bunk bed, I would literally slide from the foot end of the bed to the head of the bed and back again. This went on for two nights in a row. To me this was a part of the experience."

I hope the stories of Jeff Rea and Floyd Miller have inspired you, along with my personal story of making fitness and nutrition a priority. I encourage you to meet with a professional trainer or nutritionist to get the lowdown on what is best for you. What I have written about is what works best for me. We all are different in that respect, but the main thing is not to make excuses. I don't want to hear this stuff about, "I'm so busy" and "I have so much to do" and "Fitness Centers are expensive." Your body is a temple. It should be a priority. When you are at a decent weight and in good shape, you have a much better chance of keeping that positive attitude!

Okay, what are three action steps you are going to take from reading this chapter?

____

____

____

____

____

____

— 14 —

Tips from a Nutrition Expert

For this chapter, I sought out Dawn Meyer, a former television anchor and reporter that I have known for many years. I have witnessed her develop a passion to help people eat better, which can impact their attitude. I asked her to write this chapter on how we can take small but meaningful steps that lead to better nutrition choices.

– Charlie

BACK IN MY TELEVISION reporting days we'd be assigned a story to cover on a daily basis. Some assignments proved far more daunting than others. For example, if my news director asked me to find one person who had never once struggled with proper nutrition and diet, I might be hard pressed. Boy, would I be able to meet my five o'clock deadline? Not likely.

The simple truth is, almost every one of us struggles or has struggled with a positive attitude towards healthy nutrition. I know I have and still do! We are bombarded by convenience foods, from the grocery store to restaurants. We are busy people in a fast-paced world. It seems we are always in a hurry—work, meetings, homework, soccer.... Catching a meal "on the fly" has become a way of life. Plus, marketing these days coerces us with advertisements showing out-of-control food portions, which we have come to crave...burgers, fries, sundaes, even pancake balls with sausage inside!

The reality is that consuming fatty, sugary, enriched, processed foods makes us feel pretty crummy, groggy and slow but, more important, it can lead to serious health issues like diabetes, heart disease, high blood pressure and cholesterol—the list goes on....

We would never think of pouring sugar into our car's gas tank because we know that our car would not perform optimally. So why do we put things we know are not good for our own "engine" into our bodies? Habits are one reason. We simply become used to a certain routine that becomes comfortable and commonplace. Another is our mind. It's a powerful thing.

Since the body achieves what the mind believes, it only makes sense to try our best to become positive thinkers about the food we consume and how we consume it. It wouldn't be prudent to wake up one day and tell ourselves we are going to lose 50 pounds, exercise and stop all bad habits starting in one single day. That would be more like a diet, and diets fail most of us because we become overwhelmed and give up.

Instead, we can stay positive by tackling our goals one step at a time. Taking on the smaller hurdles first can give our minds the confidence and momentum to leap over higher ones in the future.

For example, maybe you're eating too much carry-out

and drinking too much soda. You might start by weaning yourself of sugary soft drinks and start drinking more water. As you become successful in reaching this small goal, you will no doubt feel more positive in tackling another like preparing healthier meal options in advance at home to avoid the drive thru. Build upon that and you might find time to schedule more physical activity.

As this happens, a lot of positive things begin to evolve for us. First, we feel better physically; we are less tired, have fewer aches and pains, and feel more energetic and lively. Those feelings, in turn, play a pivotal role in our mental health. We are happier, more confident, less stressed and more positive. We again command control of our body. Instead of cravings and temptations taking charge, we're the ones at the controls. How empowering is that? It gives us a more positive view of ourselves and those around us.

Maintaining those healthier habits can be arduous. Keeping a positive attitude toward our health and nutrition is essential. You've heard the saying, "We are who we hang with"? Relationships we create have a profound impact on us. Our ability to be successful and positive largely depends on the people we choose to be around. If we know people who are habitually negative, chances are we'll take on those similar traits. The same goes for positivity. If you've decided to eat more healthy and begin a fitness program, you might have to go beyond your current circle of friends to meet like-minded people—the very people who have the same goals and aspirations as you.

I conduct monthly challenge groups. Willing participants who are eager to make a change with their health, nutrition and fitness join me for 30 days. Almost all of it is conducted in a private Facebook group. We share meal plans, workout routines, and even our struggles. Everyone checks in several times on a daily basis over the month. One woman told us her husband was resistant to her healthier lifestyle and that, without the support of our group, she would have given up. Another said that it is easy enough to get off track with health and fitness without someone trying to shove her off the rails.

It is a perfect example of surrounding ourselves with like-minded people in order to make positive changes in our lives. We motivate one another, empower one another and help each other to be accountable—all because we share the same common goal.

Health, fitness or nutrition is never simply conquered—it's a journey. That's why, as a reporter with an assignment, I'd be hard pressed to find someone who has never struggled with it. Truthfully, each one of us is a work in progress.

Regardless of age, weight, occupation or social status, it is never too late to begin. One of my favorite sayings is: "Someday is not a day of the week." Turn that someday into tomorrow. It's the best gift you can give your spouse, your children and most of all..yourself!

Dawn Meyer
www.facebook.com/fitbydawn

— 15 —

Been Run Over by a Truck Lately?

I HAVE BEEN ABLE TO KEEP a positive attitude thanks, in part, to the remarkable life stories of the travelers who have gone on the group travel trips I have hosted for Edgerton's Travel. Along the way I have had many conversations with travelers about their attitudes. Most of the folks who go are in their 50s, 60s, 70s, and beyond, so they have great wisdom and insights on life and the power of the positive attitude.

We have all heard the expression, "Live each day like it will be your last. You never know, you might go out and get run over by a bus!" Edgerton's group traveler Jim Fox did just that—well, he wasn't run over by a bus, but by a truck! A few years back, Jim was all set to go on the Edgerton's Ireland trip that upcoming spring. Jim volunteers at the Morris Performing Arts Center in downtown South Bend. He loves volunteering there. On February 28, 2008, he was leaving the Morris. Someone said, "Watch it, Jim. It's slippery out there." As it turns out, ice was the least of his worries.

Jim was crossing the street. The stoplight was red,

so there was supposed to be no traffic coming his way. Suddenly, he heard someone yell, "TRUCK!!!!"

His only thought: "Oh, I'm dead."

"I never felt a thing," Jim told me. "Witnesses on the street said the big pickup truck hit me and I was on the hood and rolled off. I landed on my left shoulder and my head. As I lay there in the street, I said, 'Don't hit me.' Other cars were coming from both directions. Two cars pulled up and immediately angled themselves to block all other traffic so I would be safe. It was amazing. A beauty parlor lady from Niles, Michigan, was one of them. She put her scarf under my head. My injuries included my right pelvic bone that was broken in three places as well as shoulder and head injuries."

Jim had his priorities in line (!). What was his number one concern while lying there in the ER?? It was to see if he could still go on the 2008 Edgerton's group travel trip to Ireland!!

"In the hospital, I looked up at the Doc and said, 'Can I still go to Ireland on the Edgerton's trip?' He smiled and said that they would patch me up and I could go! I was in the hospital for 20 days and was in therapy for three months before I could drive. I did go on the Ireland trip that year and loved it." That's a case of finding a way to put some humor in a dire situation.

The man in the truck who ran over Jim took off and still has not been arrested. I asked Jim what he took away from the accident.

"You have to roll with the punches in life," Jim said. This is a man who literally rolled off the hood of a truck. "I mean, what *are* you going to do? Working out regularly really helped me. I started working out five years ago at age 73. I work out three times a week in the gym."

Having a sense of humor in life helps so much. "I joke now that when I leave the Morris I am going to need two women to walk on each side of me," said Jim, who is single.

Jim soaks up every day with a great attitude. The saying goes: "Live each day like it will be your last, because one day it will be." Jim Fox makes the most out of every precious day!

— 16 —

The Importance of Self-Talk

YOU COULD WRITE a volume of books on self-talk and its relation to positive attitude. The bottom line is to fill your mind with as many upbeat and optimistic thoughts as possible and to weed out the negative junk.

I challenge you to do this to eliminate negative self-talk. Each time you have a negative thought, stop in your tracks and make a real, real loud foghorn sound. "Ahhhh-ooooooo-guhhh!" It doesn't matter if you are in line at the grocery store, eating at a restaurant, or attending a wedding, belt it out like you are a crazy person. The embarrassment of it all will highly motivate you to avoid negative self-talk.

Seriously, while delivering my attitude seminar in Chicago, I had a lady who said she had heard a good idea was to wear a rubber band around a wrist and, when negative self-talk pops up, lift up the rubber band and pop the heck out of yourself. She had done it and said it worked!

> Hi Charlie! I heard Joel Osteen talk about "changing the channel" of our thoughts years ago and it stuck

> with me. It is a simple and effective way of stopping a negative thought flow. It's just like changing the station on a radio. Also, if there's an ongoing, serious issue that has to be dealt with (medical issue, serious family matter, career crisis, etc.), scheduling five or ten minutes every three waking hours to acknowledge the issue, talk or think about it, cry about it, plan for it, dissect it, etc., is also a great way to keep functioning throughout the rest of the days and weeks ahead. And how do you just stop giving it thought and attention after the allotted time allowance? By "changing the channel"—you know you will nurture or deal with your feelings again in a few hours, but only for a few minutes at a time. That turns the table on despair and helps to keep us functioning during the really tough times.
>
> *– Tammera Wine, private bank officer*

Here is something that has worked for me for years as far as getting my self-talk back in line (since it tends to get out of line sometimes…). There is the story of an old Cherokee chief and what he told his grandson:

> An old Cherokee chief was teaching his grandson about life..."A fight is going on inside me," he said to the boy. "It is a terrible fight and it is between two wolves. One is evil—he is anger, envy, sorrow, regret, greed, arrogance, self-pity, guilt, resentment, inferiority, lies, false pride, superiority, self-doubt, and ego. The other is good—he is joy, peace, love, hope, serenity, humility, kindness, benevolence, empathy, generosity, truth, compassion, and faith. This same fight is going on inside you—and inside every other person, too."
>
> The grandson thought about it for a minute and then asked his grandfather, "Which wolf will win?"

> The old chief simply replied, "The one you feed."

That is what it boils down to regarding self-talk: What are you feeding the most—negative or positive thoughts? Quit feeding the bad ones. Make them starve. One of the things that robs us of our positive attitude is when we conjure up "scenarios" of what might happen with most of those possibilities being negative. In that case I always think of the television show "Dragnet." It actually aired before my time—but I have seen reruns and on it Sgt. Joe Friday is regularly getting information from female informants. When they start rambling or getting off point, he always says, "Just the facts, ma'am." Save that line for your inner thoughts when you start cooking up negative possibilities.

In one of my attitude seminars out west, a lady said that when negative thoughts attack her she "sends Jesus to the door." I had another person say that they instantly visualize a giant red STOP sign. One fellow said he had read that you should picture your mind as a garden where negative thoughts are weeds—then pick them out. I had another person tell me that what worked for them was pretending they had a vacuum cleaner in their mind and, by simply turning it on, they could suck out all the negative thoughts.

What I love about delivering this seminar is getting ideas from folks! They have picked them up from places such as books and magazines. One time I was speaking in Indianapolis and a man said that he had read somewhere that you would never let someone rude come into your house and continue to be rude and obnoxious. You would see them out! He said that's the way he is with negative thoughts. He boots them out!

> Charlie, Martin Seligman's book *Learned Optimism* had a powerful effect on me. Don't take things personally, realize bad things don't last forever and consider many people are worse off. These ideas helped me in my previous profession! *– Dr. Ruth Warren*

As I wrote this book, I encouraged people to share how they stay positive. David Murrell reached out to me with some valuable tools on self-talk and how a new attitude helped turn his life around.

David told me he entered financial hardships that led to his declaring bankruptcy and David and his wife losing their home. "Early on, as all this was going on, I made a decision to look at it that God was a good God and wanted good things for me," David told me. "From that point on, I expected good things to happen. I got rid of all kinds of negative speech such as 'I'm broke.' I even started saying things then that sounded ridiculous like, 'I'm awaiting riches.' "

"I was taking a youth group to a conference," said David, "and I told myself it would be the best conference ever and that everything at the hotel would go great. My experience was the opposite. We had Mapquest issues and the church credit card wasn't accepted for almost an hour at the front desk. When I finally got to the elevator, I was ready to throw myself a pity party, but I stopped. I told myself that something like this will NOT discourage me!"

As David got back on his feet financially, he took several jobs. "I had one loading FEMA trailers," he said. "People would come to work talking about how dangerous it was to load them. I would counter with: 'It's going to be a safe day,' and 'We will be accident free.' "

David said there is a scripture in the Bible that influenced his new direction in self-talk. "It is about how bits are put into animals' mouths and it controls the direction the animal goes and how a tiny rudder controls the direction of a whole ship," he said. "I am totally paraphrasing now, but I really bought into that to the point that my self-talk is almost instinctive now. I began to change my thoughts, which changed my perspective, my behavior and my attitude."

David said he has changed other things about his life. "I want to be the person now for when my dreams come true," he said. "It is about taking it one step at a time. Another thing is investing in other people. It comes back to you and reminds you of what blessings you have and strengthens your attitude of gratitude. Finally, I don't walk in judgment of people who have been or who are in trouble. My journey softened my heart for them."

His turnaround all started with how he talked to himself.

There are several suggestions in this chapter. Write down two that you are going to put into effect immediately to make sure your self-talk is positive:

____

____

____

— 17 —

The Power of Forgiveness

BUILDING AND KEEPING a positive attitude takes work. Part of that work is reading about positive and inspirational things. I have a ritual where each week I buy the latest issue of *Sports Illustrated.* I know I could get it much cheaper as a subscription, but taking the effort to drive somewhere to get it means to me that I am serious about staying positive. In almost every issue, there is an in-depth story of courage towards the back of the magazine. The writing is so good and the stories so powerful that they reinvigorate my positive attitude.

One particular issue had the story of the remarkable positive attitude of Saundra Adams. In 1999 her daughter Cherica was carrying the child of Carolina Panthers player Rae Carruth. In a horrifying effort to prevent the birth and child support, Carruth hired two thugs to kill her and the unborn child. In a flurry of bullets into her car, they killed her; but, through a miracle, the child was born ten weeks early.

Unfortunately, seventy minutes went by from the time of the shooting to the emergency delivery. The lack of blood and oxygen to the baby's brain during that time did significant damage. Chancellor Lee was born with cerebral palsy. The story was written thirteen years later when he was mainly in a wheelchair and struggling to feed himself.

Saundra, his grandmother, is raising him. She has one of the most positive attitudes in the world. Writer Thomas Lake explained that her attitude was developed from going to Mount Olive Baptist Church as a child:

> What she learned at Mount Olive was an overwhelming sense of gratitude for life. The sense that you don't wake up unless God opens your eyes, don't see the rising sun unless God pulls it from the horizon, don't put food in your mouth unless God helps you hold the fork. And you do all these things and you rejoice.

You can only imagine what it has been like for Saundra to cope with the feelings she has for Carruth, who had her daughter murdered. Despite the tremendous grief, her attitude has been remarkable. As she explains in the article:

> Like I say, you can focus on what you've lost or what you have left.
>
> So I didn't lose. I have my grandson. I have my daughter with me in my heart, always. I have her with me through this young man. So I don't focus on loss. I mean, I think she's in Heaven, with God, so that's definitely not a loss. So I've got a lot left, and a lot of hope left and a lot to live for, and to be able to help my grandson to become the wonderful man he's meant to be. I haven't lost anything.
>
> Really, I've gained. I've been pushed into my role and destiny.

The writer, Lake, has been visibly moved by the experience of writing their story. Had Chancellor Lee had a normal birth, he probably would have grown up to be a strong athlete since his father was fast and strong. Because of the murder attempt and oxygen deprivation near birth, he has severe disabilities. His attitude, though, has been golden according to the writer:

> He is the happiest person I've ever met. There's a light inside him that I've never seen anywhere else. I've talked to several other people about his effect on me, and they say it happened to them too. Wherever he goes—to church, to physical therapy, to the Special Olympics—he makes people feel better by his mere presence. When he looks into your eyes and says hello, the whole thing feels almost spiritual. And then, of course, you have to ask yourself: If a kid like this can be so happy, what right do I have to complain?
>
> – Thomas Lake, writer,
> "The Boy They Couldn't Kill"
> *(Sports Illustrated, September 17, 2012 issue)*

That last sentence by Lake says it all... "*If a kid like this can be so happy, what right do I have to complain*?"

When we talk about attitudes, it's more than just positive. There is the "find a way" attitude. Because of his speech challenges, Chancellor Lee cannot say the word grandmother. Instead, he learned to say G-Mom. G-Mom and Chancellor are making the most of life and staying positive through forgiveness.

Ironically, as I wrote this book, another national example of forgiveness touched me and thousands more. Josh Brent of the Dallas Cowboys was accused of driving under the influence in an accident that killed his teammate and best friend Jerry Brown. They had been college teammates at the University of Illinois. In a remarkable gesture of forgiveness and caring about others in the midst of grief, Stacey Jackson, who is Jerry Brown's mother, reached out to the driver Josh Brent. She invited him to sit with her during the funeral of her son. He was a son who died obviously because of Brent's poor driving after being under the influence.

"I know he is hurting just as much as we are," she told CNN. "[He] and Jerry were like brothers. I was upset, but I realized that our youth today are young and stupid, and we were all once that age, and we've all done things we're not proud of." While she was going through indescribable grief, she found it within her to think about how much Josh was hurting over losing his great friend.

There are giants when it comes to forgiveness. After the horrific shootings at Sandy Hook Elementary School in Connecticut, Robbie Parker said something that moved me and many others deeply. His six-year-old daughter Emilie was among those killed. Despite his overwhelming grief, he also thought about the family of the killer. "I can't imagine how hard this experience must be for you," he said. "Our love and support goes out to you as well."

It is very hard and almost impossible to keep a positive attitude if there is someone we need to forgive in our life. But if we don't forgive, the anger and hard feelings will boil up from time to time and suck the joy out of what could be a fulfilling and optimistic life.

There are some cases in your life where the hurt is deep and to forgive seems very hard, but I hope that the examples in this chapter will give you the strength you need.

Who do you need to forgive in your life?

____

____

____

____

____

What are you going to do about it?

____

____

____

____

____

____

____

____

____

— 18 —

Even the Best of Us Can Lose Our Positive Attitude!

KEEPING THAT DARN positive attitude is tough. I have seen some of the most optimistic people in world history get down, myself included.Back in my television news days, I reported on the Notre Dame football program for many years. They had a player named Jerome "the Bus" Bettis who was and is one of the most positive people anywhere! Bettis always has a big smile on his face and companies pay him to endorse their products—partly because he was a successful pro football player and also because he comes across in such an upbeat manner.

There was a time when Bettis was not positive. After starring at Notre Dame for Coach Lou Holtz, he was drafted by the St. Louis Rams. In his book *A Teen's Game Plan for Life*, Holtz shares the story of how, by Bettis' third season with the Rams, he was playing poorly and some thought he wouldn't make it in the pros despite having massive talent. Bettis was part of a

Rams team that was losing and, in any culture like that, your attitude can take a hit. Well, Holtz watched one of his games on television, saw him play like a shell of his former self, and then called him up not long after the game. He told Bettis that he had seen the Rams play and that some guy was impersonating him and wearing his jersey and number. He said the guy was giving Bettis a bad name and that he had to find a way to stop it. He then hung up the phone.

As Holtz describes it, Bettis went back to Notre Dame after the pro season and visited Holtz. Bettis told him that, when he left Notre Dame, he had a wonderful attitude but that he had let it go down in the pros. Isn't that ironic? He was making millions of dollars as a pro but his attitude was bad. When he was poor growing up in Detroit, he had a good attitude. Bettis then told Holtz he was going to stay on campus for four months and work on his attitude. He did and ended up as one of the best running backs in pro football history.

There are three things that we all have to do at some point or points in our life:

(1) admit that our attitudes have gone sour;
(2) do what it takes to turn them around;
(3) reap the benefits of a rejuvenated positive attitude.

I once worked in television news with a reporter that started his career as one of the most upbeat and vibrant people I had ever seen. He came to work every day with zip in his step and he loved his job. He used to be able to get a camera and go out and put together features of people for the evening newscast. Sure, there were headaches and challenges in his job, but there are in any position. What happened, though, was that he started focusing on the negatives. He started to see that other reporters got a camera person to work with them in the field and that he was having to do the camera work on his own. He then started harping over the vehicle he had to drive for assignments and how other crews had new news cars. Slowly, a toxic negative attitude started to seep into his inner attitude core. I had someone from the newsroom come to me and say that he was saying negative things about others and that it was an issue. I tried to talk with him but his attitude was so negative that it was out of control. The manager of the newsroom came to me and said they were going to fire him, basically because of attitude. They did and what once was a dream job for him was now a vapor.

Several months after that, I got a call from an employer very interested in hiring him for a position that would put him in front of others. At first I was reluctant to endorse him because of the attitude, but I am a firm believer in second chances and know well that an attitude can be improved. I had heard his attitude had been improved at other positions so I supported him in his new opportunity. He got the job and turned out to be a great hire. Like Jerome Bettis, he had an attitude shift. He rebuilt the darn thing and has kept it ever since.

Be frank with yourself about your attitude. Where does your attitude stink?

What are you going to do about it?

— 19 —

Encouragement

IT IS AMAZING WHAT a sincere gesture of encouragement can do for one's positive attitude.

Here is a story of how ten encouraging words were the difference in someone finishing or quitting their first marathon. While I was speaking on attitude for a company in Phoenix, I asked for a volunteer to illustrate a point. Karen Murray volunteered and then promptly hobbled up to where I was standing. She moved gingerly because she had run a 26.2-mile marathon the day before.

As one who studies high achievers, I was curious as to how Karen got past "The Wall," that part of a marathon that feels like you have run into a wall. The story she shared with me gives me goosebumps about the fire that we have within us...and about the power of encouraging words!

Karen had run three half-marathons, but this was to be her first full one. Going into the run, she had prepped herself for how hard this would be. She went through three months of training every other day for three miles and one day each weekend for up to 18 miles. Karen thought about how much she hurt when she did her first half-marathon and prepared herself for double the pain. She was okay with knowing she would experience pain. For her it was all about finishing and getting that medal that said "Marathon," not "Half-Marathon."

The night before the run Karen dreamt that she was the last person to finish. When she got to her corral, it was #11—the last one...not much of a morning motivator. The race began. She felt great when she finished the first six miles right at an hour! She had been stressing about keeping a good time all through training as she normally runs 12-minute miles, so averaging a 10-minute mile was a huge motivator!

The next big milestone was the half-marathon marker! Her only thoughts were that she felt so good that she wouldn't have a problem getting through this.... Then at mile 18, a tendon in her knee popped. She went down! The medic station was nearby and the paramedic wrapped her leg as best he could and off she went. She thought to herself, "Maybe if I walk one mile and run the next I will be okay...the pain was *so* intense." But, she kept on running!

By mile 21, every muscle and bone in her body felt as though someone threw her down and kicked every inch of her body. Karen was wracked with pain from head to toe. She could feel the blisters on her feet getting bigger and bigger. She looked down at her hands and arms and they were so swollen you couldn't see one line in her hand, or even one knuckle. She had to loosen her watch two holes because it was so tight. Karen really didn't know how she would get through the next 5 miles.

All of these thoughts were going through her mind as she came upon the water station. At the end of the water station she glanced over at a man with no legs who was handing her a glass of water. He said to her, "You're doing a great job....Keep up the good work!"

At that point Karen's body didn't hurt so badly anymore! She didn't care about the swollen hands and the blister pain seemed to disappear. She picked up that hurt leg and finished that marathon, to the very best of her ability—without thoughts of pity—thanks to the man with no legs!

> What an awesome experience and a commitment to a lifetime achievement completing a marathon is for me! Five years ago I ran my first mile and competitive 5K. This year I ran my first marathon! A marathon! Me, who couldn't run one mile without walking five years ago. Me, I finished a marathon! It is still hard to believe how perseverance always prevails!
>
> – Karen Murray

The encouragement from that volunteer was the difference. That is the power of encouragement! It doesn't cost a thing to give and yet it is priceless to receive. George Adams once said, "Encouragement is the oxygen to the soul."

Here is a personal example of the power of encouragement in keeping a positive attitude. I have delivered many Talks over the past twenty-five years to all kinds of audiences. In every case I find those in the audience who are nodding regularly to my points. While I make a point to try to look at everyone, I keep glancing at that woman or man whose head is bobbing up and down to my points. I feed off that encouragement. It keeps me positive about my message. I don't care who you are as a speaker. There are folks in every audience who don't want to be there, probably because of their negative attitude. They usually look like they are sucking on a lemon. Instead, I gravitate to the nodders because encouragement is vital to have—and to give out—when it comes to positive attitude.

This book as well as my keynotes and seminars on attitude are not just built on how you build and keep your positive attitude. If we make an effort to create an environment of positivity, then we sure have a better chance of keeping our positive attitude. A big part of that is through encouragement.

There is a fine line between going over the top with encouragement and giving out just the right amount. I remember when I was in television news and one time Richard Simmons came to our station for an on-air appearance. I could hear him down the hall because he was so wound up and positive. Now, I get his impact and think the world of how he has impacted so many people but, when people are too zippy, that makes even me a bit unsettled. If someone walks in a room and says, "Hey, Bob, you are terrific. Jane! You are so special! Mort, you are A-#1! Oh, there is Roberta, the jewel of life!" Okay, no one goes that overboard, but you get my gist. The key with encouragement is to make it sincere and personal. That can do wonders for someone's attitude and makes you feel good in the process. Proverbs 11:25 makes that clear: "He who refreshes others will himself be refreshed." Hebrews 10:24-25 shares the value of encouragement: "And let us consider how we may spur one another on toward love and good deeds. Let us not give up meeting together, as some are in the habit of doing, but let us encourage one another—and all the more as you see the Day approaching."

Encouragement gives people a greater sense of self-value. I have always loved this approach: "Pretend everyone has a sign around them that reads 'Make me feel Important' " (Mary Kay). If there is one thing I learned by being around over half a century, it is that people truly love acknowledgment. It doesn't mean all at once, but at the appropriate time.

Tool for you: Take the time now or over the next twenty-four hours to have a signature quote at the end of your email messages that pertains to attitude. It can be under your contact information. Find a quote that you like and put it there and it will no doubt perk up someone who reads your email. It's a little thing that can help. Building and keeping a positive attitude and helping others to do the same is a combination of many little things.

Who is one person in your life that you can encourage today by a personal visit, phone call or note?

____

____

____

—20—

"Delicious, as Always!"

TWENTY YEARS AGO I WAS DELIVERING a form of my motivational keynote "Stoke the Fire Within" at an Assembly at Riley High School in South Bend. I went in the normal way, by...walking.

Not Captain Ed Friend.

He rode his rumbling Police motorcycle down the halls of the school and into the gymnasium where the students roared loudly!

I was like, "Whoa! Now *THAT'S* an entrance!"

Ed died in the spring of 2012 at the age of 75. As they say, it's not how many years you live, but how much life you put into your years. Ed put 150 into his life. When I heard he died my immediate thought was that the world had lost a really special guy and one who was truly one of a kind. He had one of the most positive attitudes in the world!

One of the main points of the "Stoke the Fire Within" keynote is the lesson the gruff TV-News cameraman taught me in October of 1991 regarding the attitude of

doing our job the best way possible. I wanted to do a TV-News live shot at the top of the steps of the Philadelphia Museum of Art and reference the Rocky Balboa statue behind me during the live report. He wouldn't let me. He insisted we lay enough cable to start the shot at the bottom of the steps and run all 70-plus steps to the top, just like Rocky has done in the movies. It turned out to be an amazing live report!

My point to audiences is that you can live your life in a tripod way, where you are solid and all that—or you can "run the steps"!

Ed Friend ran the steps, especially when it came to positive attitude.

From his distinctive bow ties to his constant smile, this man lived a truly unique life. He was a police officer in South Bend for almost half a century. Some say he was the most popular officer of all time. He cared deeply for the elderly and for the kids. He was a driving force behind the local Crime Stoppers program. He developed all kinds of programs for the elderly and the kids. Ed created a TV show called "Kids Adventure Zone" that rocked on Saturday mornings! He asked me to be on it one time about 15 years ago. My father happened to be visiting so I took him to the studio. Ed made my dad feel like a million bucks. He went out of his way to make him welcome. When the show started, Ed engaged the kids like he was a professional TV host, in addition to a Police Captain.

As someone who was in television for almost a quarter of a century, I know how hard it is to produce and host programs. Ed made it look easy, and he was a policeman by trade!

Ed cared deeply about his work with the Police Department. He got married to Jane at 10:30 in the morning back on a crisp fall morning in 1962. By 2:30 that afternoon, he was back at work (she must have been cool with that as they were married 50 years).

In his later years, he transitioned to writing about seniors. He had a way of inspiring people to have a positive attitude with a regular column he created called "Friend's Advice." One of the columns got me so keyed up that I have kept it handy for years. It was about a positive 95-year-old woman named Gladys Sheneman who was active "as all get-out" as my Uncle Everett would say.

This is what Ed wrote about Gladys for his local paper, the *South Bend Tribune*:

> She just turned 95 this past July and is on the go all the time. Gladys is the den mother of momentum. Age is a numerical equation for accomplishment or despair. Retirement is a word that should never have been invented or pursued. I have known people at age 35 so bored with life that they had one foot in the grave counting the hours, days, months and years until they could retire. I have known other folks who had no plans to leave their jobs, ever.
>
> She developed a band several years ago. She plays

> piano and her colleagues accompany her on quaint instruments such as the washboard, gut bucket and other novel tune makers. The band plays at the North Liberty American Legion Post the first Friday of each month at lunch time.
>
> Gladys has been president of Retired Neighbors and Friends for 17 years. The group meets at Pine Creek Church the second Tuesday of each month and about 150 achievers gather each month for lunch. Her band plays there, too. She has told them when they see her start "losing her marbles, tell her" but they haven't told her yet. So, she retains the presidency.
>
> Her faith in God is credited for her good health. She recently walked a mile-and-a-half trail at Potato Creek "just like when I was a girl" she told me. Her wish: When the Lord calls her home, she wants to be in her own home, no hospital!
>
> *by Ed Friend*

I loved the part about Gladys telling her friends, "Hey, when you see me start to lose my marbles, oust me as President!" I think we should all adopt that approach!

Ed lived an extraordinary life. He became a really good public speaker, and spoke at my Church just a few years ago. Our Pastor, Dr. Pat Somers, had many conversations with him over the years. I asked him to reflect on those...

> Charlie, I was struck that Ed Friend had such a positive spirit. We spoke on several occasions about how the essence of faith uplifts and encourages. He had a passion for people—all people, young or old, which he conveyed to our congregation when he was guest

speaker a few years back. I was privileged to join him in prayer on several occasions. I will miss him.

– *Pastor Pat, Evangel Heights United Methodist Church*

Just a few years ago, Ed reflected on his life in a lengthy interview with the *South Bend Tribune*, and summarized it this way: "I don't think I could sleep soundly at night if I couldn't look back on the day and not be able to recall at least one person I had helped."

That is a key to building and keeping a positive attitude. Ed went into each day with an approach of service to others. That filled him with joy and a state of being content. After his death, people expressed how Ed made a difference:

"My mother was a widow living in her home in South Bend, and I was in Texas. I had heard she fell and broke her hip, and I called Ed long distance about her and he was at her house in a moment with an ambulance to get her to the hospital."

"Ed, you will be missed. My son Riley is a Marine today because of your suggestion when we ran into my old friend one day at the Farmers Market. He called as soon as he saw of your passing. You have impacted so many lives!!!!! What a legacy you have left!"

"I first met Ed decades ago when my son's bike was stolen. Ed had the bike in his office and carried it to my car. He was so nice to deal with."

"Ed showed all of us how to live our lives and I have not lost sight of those lessons. It is not about money, it is about service and I will carry that until I die."

"I think what I will miss most was his sparkling eyes and radiant smile when I would ask how he was doing and he smiled his smile and said, 'Delicious, as always!' We'll miss you, Friend."

The next time today that someone asks how you are doing, you may want to answer, "Delicious, as always!" Do it with a twinkle in your eyes....

—21—

A Positive-Attitude Workplace Environment

I AM GOING TO SHARE an example of how one business has created a positive attitude in their workplace and a spirit of service to the customer. I had been hearing about McCormick Electrical Services in North Liberty, Indiana, for years so I called them up and said I was coming over to produce a video on them to share in my attitude seminars. Tom McCormick is the president and welcomed me to spend a day with them.

It was a Monday morning. I arrived for their early morning meeting. Outside the conference room door was a sign that read: "If you are late for a meeting, you owe the team $5." That money would go to charity or a company social event. I really liked that idea. I realize some people have reasons for being late, but it creates a negative vibe if people stroll into meetings late. Here's another idea to not just make people on time but to keep meetings on task. Keep them standing up. I know some meetings are going to go long and you can't do that, but

I assure you that standing up would lead to the other meetings to remaining on task.

In many cases their electricians are at the client's home going over their electrical needs. As their meeting started, I saw a sign that had all of the positive attitude attributes they wanted to show in front of clients:

* Smile * speak cheerfully * eye contact * compliment
* listening * concern * give options * respect

Tom then shared the customer evaluation cards from the previous week. "The most important thing to most of our customers was employee attitude," Tom said. "It says here 'Nick was very professional and very nice when he came to our house. I was most impressed with his attitude. I wish he could work for me!' "

Tom McCormick leads his employees through a ten-minute attitude training session early each Monday morning. On the day I was there they watched a few minutes of the DVD "Gaining and Maintaining a Mountain Mover Attitude." They each had a workbook in which they took notes and then they had a discussion for about four minutes. "One of the things I am going to do this week is say at least three nice things a day and focus on laughing at myself more," said one employee during that discussion.

Tom has two shelves of positive attitude books on his office shelf that employees can check out. He even has a Dewey Decimal System for them. Tom also told me that, whenever he goes to electrical conferences, he always takes notes on what the motivational speaker says at each one. He then shares those notes during the Monday morning meeting. During the meeting I could see why his employees have such a good attitude as he told them he considered them an extension of his family.

After the meeting they showed me their fish. Tom has a program where, if someone in the office sees someone helping someone else or going above and beyond, they make sure that person is awarded a paper fish. Each employee has a "stringer" to keep their fish on and every so often they have a fishing derby. They bring in their fish and the one with the most fish gets a prize.

As their meeting started to wind down, they went over customer service again and the workers showed me the foot coverings they wear in the customers' homes. "We leave the home cleaner than when we arrived," said one, showing me the mini-vacuum cleaner they take inside. I also learned that they wear uniforms that are dry cleaned before each day. "The workers seem to stand three inches taller when they put them on," said Tom, talking about how their attitude is lifted upon wearing crisp clean uniforms each day. They also wear white-collared shirts. "It goes back to the cowboy westerns," said Tom. "Good guys wear white. Our studies show that customers are much more relaxed and positive when an electrician arrives wearing white."

As we moved back into their garage area they showed me the Darts for Dollars board. If an employee meets a revenue goal for the week, they get to throw a dart at a board that has a fifty dollar bill folded near the bull's-eye. If they hit it, they keep it! They showed me the positive-attitude CDs they have in the vehicles that were provided for the electricians to listen to (if they wanted to) while driving to homes.

Tom then pulled out a coin from his pants pocket. "It reads 'the future you live tomorrow is the future you build today,' " said Tom. "What I do, say and interpret today affects my and our future. Another thing I focus on is that I am accountable to a higher power—that being God, that being Christ. A friend of mine in business has a portrait in his office of an executive at a desk sitting across from Christ. It makes me realize that in everything I do with a client, I am accountable to God."

Before leaving, I spoke with Donna. She runs the office. Extremely positive, she told me how she loves talking to customers on the phone. "I get to hear their special stories," she said. "If they have had a bad day, I listen. That means a lot to them."

The video I produced of their positive-attitude workplace runs about seven minutes and I play it in the "How to Build a Positive Attitude and KEEP the Darn Thing!!" seminar that I deliver. Many organizations have taken ideas from it and put them to work at their place.

What are three things from what McCormick does that you can do in your workplace?

____

____

____

—22—

Keeping a Positive Attitude at Work

IN MY DAYS as a positive-attitude reporter at WSBT-TV, I once did a story on a lady who was a custodian for a local elementary school. On the surface her job would be to keep the school clean for everyone. That's a huge job and a critical one because, without custodians, places would be a mess. Well, Marcia Elsbury went way beyond her job description and, when I met her, I found her to be SO positive! Besides cleaning, she also read books to the students in classrooms, took parts in plays, dressed up as the Easter bunny, brought in treats and all kinds of things. I remember the principal saying that she went way beyond her job description. One teacher told me that Marcia was the kind that initiated things. You might be thinking, "Well, how did she have time to do all of this with all of her cleaning duties?" I got the answer when I interviewed her for the feature. She said that, because she got to know the kids so much better, she hardly ever had messes. They kept things way cleaner than normal! They loved her positive attitude and giving spirit. When I talked to her she said she didn't look at the kids as just students. She considered them her grandkids. She told me those kids had a mountain of love to give and she loved to receive it and give it back to them. She loved her job!

We will spend a lot of hours at work so it is critical to fortify our positive attitude in that environment. Over the years I have learned that it is very important to take pride in your job, even though it may not seem like one of the premier jobs. Most of us will not be company presidents or even department heads, but we all can care about our jobs.

Nick Saban is viewed as the top college football coach in the country. The Alabama head coach has his team in the national championship hunt just about every year. Several years ago, I was the emcee of an event where he spoke at the College Football Hall of Fame. The one thing that I took away from his talk and still remember today is his quote from Dr. Martin Luther King, Jr.:

> If a man is called to be a street sweeper, he should sweep streets even as Michelangelo painted, or Beethoven composed music, or Shakespeare wrote poetry. He should sweep streets so well that all the hosts of heaven and earth will pause to say, "Here lived a great street sweeper who did his job well."

Saban talked about how Dr. King really only wanted one man to shine his shoes and that was this fellow outside the Green Stamp Store in Montgomery, Alabama. Why? Because the guy did a great job, loved his craft, did it with a smile on his face, and showed appreciation when he was thanked for doing an excellent job.

For 23 years I was a sports anchor at television stations in Meridian, Mississippi; Bakersfield, California; South Bend,

Indiana; and New Orleans, Louisiana. I can relate to the quote above because the sports anchor was at the bottom of the totem pole when it came to television news priorities. There was News and there was Weather and way after that was Sports. What I did was often viewed as the "toy department" of the news and customarily was given the shortest amount of time. I usually had to do my own video camera work out in the field, my own editing and often had my sports-segment time cut drastically if the rest of the News was running long.

Still, I took great pride in my work and, as a result, felt satisfaction. My attitude was positive because of that approach.

My cousin Richard Lowe (who, like me, is in his early 50s and has been around the block) shared his thoughts with me on caring about your work—no matter how mundane others may perceive it to be—and how it impacts your attitude. This is dead on:

> Rachel [his girlfriend] and I were talking recently about why so many people seem to accept "good enough," as if simply completing a task adequately with minimum expenditure of energy is the objective. The quicker and easier the solution to, say, mopping a floor, is preferable to caring about the quality of our work. Of course mopping to most people is a mundane task to be dispatched with as expeditiously as possible, like doing the laundry, or taking out the garbage, or mowing the lawn. But when mopping is necessary, there is a way to elevate it to become something redeeming.
>
> If I choose to *care* about the quality of my work, I will consider it a challenge to learn something every time I do it: How does the amount of

water I squeeze out of the mop affect cleaning this floor? Does it make a difference that loose strands are dangling eight inches below the body of the mop head? Would it help in any way to trim these stragglers? Is there a more effective way to section this floor in my mind to make sure every square inch has been mopped well? Does it make an appreciable difference to change the water after each mopping?

These questions are driven by both curiosity and caring. Taking pride in the quality of our work brings with it an enormous measure of freedom and satisfaction. It's not about being a perfectionist; sometimes the challenge is with time—to finish the job adequately in a very finite space of time. Then it becomes a matter of efficiency and pacing and discipline. The job becomes a healthy challenge because I *make* it a healthy challenge. Otherwise it's just drudgery at a hurried pace.

Is it possible to cultivate this attitude in others? I strive to model this state of mind and action to the clients I teach, who overwhelmingly see mopping as a job to just get done, with minimal caring involved; to make some money. To the degree this attitude is exercised, we are slaves to such tasks. To the degree we care and take pride in the quality of our work, we are the masters of them.

Even in the mundane—especially in the mundane—we are presented with opportunities to challenge ourselves and. in doing so, to contribute satisfaction, healthy pride, and integrity into our soul's account. I think of it as the mortar [attitude] which holds the bricks [accomplishment] together. The quality of that mortar is entirely in my hands.

– Richard Lowe

The thing that I did that allowed me to stay positive in very challenging work situations was this: I did my job for my customers and my co-workers, not for my company. Not that I didn't care about the parent company, but over time just about anyone will realize they are expendable within a company or organization. By focusing on serving others (customers) and working for your teammates (your co-workers), you will find that you can stay pretty darn positive. The key word here is "serve" your customers. When you dedicate yourself to helping others through your job, it is only natural to be more positive than someone who comes in "to work." As far as your co-workers, I understand there are those who drive you half batty, but you have those you care about and, when you are working for them, it makes you more positive.

> Charlie, every worker wants to be told they're doing a good job. A negative attitude begins when workers are not noticed when they are going above and beyond. Nowadays, it's mostly not the pay that creates the positive attitude, so it's appreciation that is vital. A negative attitude is created when a boss is obsessed with focusing on the negative. A boss's attitude directly affects the attitude of their employees. I am a firm believer in cross-training when at all possible as this builds respect for your co-worker.
>
> – *Brenda Harpster*

To keep your darn positive attitude at work, you have to realize you will face challenges each day that could take it away. The key is rising above those challenges. In 2012, I hosted an Edgerton's group travel trip to New Mexico for their famous International Balloon Fiesta. It was an amazing experience. One morning we were among over one hundred hot air balloons that rose majestically up into the skies. All around us were hot air balloons of different designs. One looked like Darth Vader. Another was a zebra. There were bumblebee balloons. As we were up there, I thought about positive attitude and how we have to rise above certain things. Visualize yourself as a hot air balloon of the design of your choice, and see yourself rising above being a part of gossip and saying negative things about others. Picture yourself up there with a cool breeze in your face and far beneath you is being jealous of a co-worker. Pretend you have found a positive wind current and nothing is going to bring you out of it.

We all have had or are going to have difficult people to work with in life. There are some real humdingers out there, as I like to say. Rather than getting all bent out of shape, one way to deal with that is to tell yourself that you will grow from having to work with this person. If anything, it will make you stronger. Dig deep for compassion for them. There could be great hurt in their life. Try to see the good. Communicate where you have differences. Don't rub in how positive you are. Tone it down a bit, but still keep the positive glow. Give it time. Pray about it.

Scott Franko is the president of U.S. Signcrafters. They are in their 21st year of business and now have five interrelated business divisions that work together to help clients with their branding and image.

> Charlie, I found writing and sharing it with others to be my way of keeping a positive attitude. I started writing when I became the sign company

> president. Every Friday, on pay-day, I wrote a "note from the company to the employees" that was given to the employees with their paychecks. They continue today but they are now distributed by email. Hence, the pay-day notes became known as and called "Pay Notes." The messages center around how to catch and maintain a positive attitude, how to be a team, and how to achieve more at work and in life. They challenge, motivate, and provoke thought. The first Pay Note was called "Living Happily with Worn-Out Shoes" and that became the first chapter of the first published book of Pay Notes which has now been printed three times. I would have never guessed that a simple note would help to foster the positive changes in our company or become a book.

Scott came up with ten attributes for improvement, performance, and accomplishment. He says the first is...Attitude.

> Charlie, attitude comes from within and expresses your true state of being. Everything you say and do is an extension of your attitude, which can be positive or negative. Attitude directly affects your motivation, and both attitude and motivation can be influenced from the outside. Fortunately, you have the ultimate power to decide whether you will trust your inner being or external influences. You can also choose whether your attitude will be positive or negative.
>
> It is wise to train your attitude to stand up to the negative forces that will attack it. You must guard it carefully. This ability comes from training. When you develop the control necessary to maintain a positive attitude, your mind and body will follow with the choices and actions that will help you achieve tremendous results.

Your attitude is the intersection of the mind, body, and soul. Belief, faith, and hope are branches that grow out of a healthy, positive attitude. A positive attitude is mightier than any instrument, for with it you can change the outcome of a situation independently. It's even possible to change the mindset of the people around you, because a positive attitude can be perceived and contains the power of persuasion.

Your attitude influences outcomes. It is able to overcome defeat and lift you up in victory. In life, sometimes you will win; sometimes you will lose. Either way, your attitude should be that of a champion and contain genuine thankfulness in order to achieve happiness and peace. You will never know your true limits or potential for achievement until you unleash a purely positive attitude to guide your thoughts and actions.

Attitude is the attribute that forms the foundation for the others. As the recipient of this attribute, you have a responsibility to treasure it, apply it, and share it with others.

– Scott Franko, author of
Lessons from an Old Pair of Gloves

Charlie, recognizing each other's strengths and weaknesses and having a morning huddle helps our small office to run like a well-oiled machine.

– Anne Nowak Borrelli, works in a Dentist office

—23—

One More Thing, One More Time

ONE OF MY GOALS is to be in the best physical shape of my life now that I have passed 50 years of age. When I am working out, I will regularly tell myself, "One more thing. One more time." That's because I made the effort to go see a remarkable speaker who helped me fortify my positive attitude and who gave me a quote that I use to this day.

When I learned that the Logan Center in my community was bringing in Paralympics ski racer and author of *Just Don't Fall*, Josh Sundquist, to be the keynote speaker at their annual event, I made it a priority to be there to hear his positive message. As I sat and heard his talk, I had a small notebook with me and took notes. I wanted to write down certain things he said because I knew they would help me keep my positive attitude. When you go to hear speakers, take a notepad. You don't have to write everything, but when something really connects with you, jot down a few words.

Josh was diagnosed with a rare form of bone cancer

at age 9. Given a 50/50 shot at living, he underwent intense chemo and had his entire left leg amputated. By 13, he was cured of cancer. At 16, he took up skiing. And at age 22, he earned a spot on the U.S. Paralympic Ski Team for the 2006 Paralympics in Italy.

"I have dealt with this through humor," he told us. "Not that every bad thing is hilarious and has a silver lining, but when things happen, you can choose how you respond."

For a while he had a prosthetic leg. He said people would come up to him and look at the leg and ask if the foot was fake too (!). He would pause and tell them of the amazing technology where they can take your real foot and sew it to your artificial leg!

Josh eventually gave up the prosthetic leg and has since made it on one leg and arm crutches. He told the hilarious story of when he was a younger man and his buddies decided to go to the movies. Because movie-theater food is expensive, they smuggled in some snacks. A friend decided that a 2-liter of Coke would be good, so they decided to put regular pants on Josh and put the 2-liter bottle in Josh's empty pant leg. They tied a knot at the knee, causing the movie theater people to think he was a man with half a leg and not one missing an entire leg. This caper would have worked except that when Josh moved toward the ticket line on his crutch-type device, the "leg" with the 2-liter bottle of Coke in it started swinging like crazy. It wouldn't stop. The ticket taker just looked at him....

While funny and upbeat, Josh said he has days when

he is down like the rest of us. Yes, motivational speakers are not zippity-doo-dah all the day long.

"There are days where everything is falling apart," he said. "The best hope at times like that is to ask for the courage to stand and the strength to walk. Whatever happens, keep hope alive."

Earlier in this book, I wrote about the Four Needs that, if met, can help us to be content. Josh said the U.S. Paralympic Ski Coach gave him a shot at making the U.S. team, and that gave him hope. It gave him opportunity and a purpose. That is one of the Four Needs. At age 16, he was not a good skier. To think that at 22 he would make the U.S. Paralympic team was not very realistic.

"I took the approach of **1MT, 1MT,**" he said of the ferocious work ethic he developed to make the team. "One more thing. One more time. Because sometimes the difference between success and failure or first and second is simply doing one more thing, one more time."

He talked about the toughest walk in his life. He was nine years old when he walked on two legs for the final time—into the room where the doctors would amputate an entire leg. Imagine that feeling as he knew that within a short time he would never again walk on two legs.

The best walk in his life? When he walked in wearing USA as part of the U.S. team at the Paralympics Games in Italy as 30,000 people cheered. He said it was an incredible feeling. It happened because when he was tired of practicing, he would remember 1MT, 1MT, and he would practice a ski move one more time.

"If I could go back all those years," he said, "what

advice would I give to myself as a nine-year-old thinking there was no hope? I had cancer and couldn't play soccer like I used to. I had always dreamed of wearing a shiny Travel Team soccer uniform, but that wasn't going to happen. What advice would I have given myself...? I would have said, 'No matter what happens, keep hope alive.' "

—24—

The Most Powerful Attitude Quote Ever

BECAUSE I WRITE AND SPEAK on attitude and motivation, I find myself sometimes assuming that people already know certain quotes that are powerful. That's not always the case. I was hosting an Edgerton's group travel trip to Charleston/Savannah one time when several people from the group of fifty came up to me in a restaurant. Knowing my passion for motivation and positive attitude, they brought me these small cards that the restaurant had sitting near their salt and pepper shakers. The restaurant owner must have been into motivation.

The cards had the quote by Chuck Swindoll that I think is one of the greatest, if not *the* greatest, quote on how important attitude is in life. What surprised me was that most of these people had never read the quote. These were accomplished professionals. So, if they hadn't seen it, I assumed that many others had not read it either. Here it is:

> The longer I live, the more I realize the impact of attitude on life. Attitude, to me, is more important than facts. It is more important than the past, than education, than money, than circumstances, than failures, than successes, than what other people think or say or do. It is more important than appearance, giftedness or skill. It will make or break a company...a church...a home. The remarkable thing is we have a choice every day regarding the attitude we will embrace for that day. We cannot change our past...we cannot change the fact that people will act in a certain way. We cannot change the inevitable. The only thing we can do is play on the one string we have, and that is our attitude. I am convinced that life is 10% what happens to me and 90% how I react to it. And so it is with you...we are in charge of our attitudes.
>
> – *Charles Swindoll*

That quote is huge. As I tell company and organizational leaders, attitude is everything! Swindoll nails it on the head.

Attitude is more important than education. Yes, I know that those in the engineering, medical and legal fields could argue the importance of education there, but I have seen plenty of people—especially in the medical profession—with terrible attitudes.

Attitude will make or break a company, church or home. That is powerful stuff there and it is right on line. In speaking for twenty-five years, most requests I get from meeting planners boil down to attitude and their need to make sure their people are as positive as possible. Homes can absolutely be destroyed by attitude. If one spouse starts focusing on the negatives of the other, look out. Churches that become divisive on issues and don't have loving attitudes suddenly find many of their members darting off to other churches.

The power of choice. This is all pretty simple. Choose positive thoughts. Choose to be optimistic. Choose to be solution centered. We are not born winners. We are not born losers. We are born choosers. The choices we make regarding our attitudes are huge.

Life is 10% what happens to us and 90% how we react to it. You are going to get knocked down. You will have politics at work that make you madder than a wet hen. A major health challenge or challenges will hit you. Life will not be fair. The question is, how are you going to react? Better yet, how will you respond?

As I wrote this book, I encouraged regular folks like you and me to contribute insights on attitude. Here are more of them:

> Hi, Charlie! If I find myself with a bad attitude, I acknowledge it and allow it—but hopefully never cling to it for more than a few minutes. Then I let it go...like an injured butterfly...hoping it heals. The more I practice, the easier it is to release negativity and put kindness and compassion back in its place.
>
> – *Tammera Wine*
>
> I used to be the most positive person anyone could meet. Then the economy took a fall and it was really hard to keep a good attitude when everything you work for is being taken right out from under you. When I get too down about everything though, God lifts me back up. If it weren't for God, not sure what I would do.
>
> – *Tammy Venable*

Charlie, the people that I see who have the best attitude are those who are going through a crisis and still want to serve others!

– Carrie Windsor Cannon

My gratitude attitude is deeply rooted in my faith. For me, the best way to "keep the darn thing" is to give it away. It's not that I'm "Miss Susie Sunshine" every day, but I am a human fighting battles just like every other human. Because I know where and from whom my happiness comes, my hope always is to be able to help someone who has not yet found their gratitude attitude to find it. If I'm having a day (like this one) where my gratitude attitude is buried somewhere in pain meds, I pray. That probably sounds like a slick answer, but it works for me. I ask my awesome God to forgive my yuk attitude and help me live outside the pain. I do something constructive (for me, that's following my passion of encouragement writing). God's faithfulness never ceases to amaze me...and it never will.

– Mary Ellen Shedron

When something unfortunate happens I always try to think of five or ten things that could have happened instead that would have been worse. This changes my perspective in the moment and makes me feel grateful. It is not cancer, it is not a head injury, no one died...

– Mary Zeisz Dunfee

Every day I have a choice on how my day will go. Will I use it to positively affect other people? Or will I complain about minor woes that don't really matter? In my mind, negativity is a form of evil and I avoid it whenever I can.

– Beth Erwin Davis

How can your attitude be better at work or where you are being educated?

___

___

___

___

___

___

___

___

___

___

—25—

Overcoming the Worst Stretch of My Life

I HAVE ALWAYS BEEN TOLD that I have a positive attitude. When I was in television news, I had thousands of viewers tell me this: "We watch you because of your enthusiasm and the way you put a positive perspective on things." Television station management came to me and showed me how ratings research showed that the viewers responded to my positive attitude. That's what led to me being a positive news reporter for years and being able to do the television features that I use in my positive attitude seminars and keynotes.

Like you, I have had challenges in life. My attitude has been knocked around and, while I have become negative at times, I have always been able to stay positive because of the things I write about in this book. I did want to share with you a story of the time in my life when I was at my lowest point, and how I was able to keep a positive attitude then. I know many of you have gone through a brutally hard time or may go through one someday. In this chapter, I wanted to share how you can emerge victoriously.

Just past my mid-40s, I was given the 1-2 punch of learning that my eyesight was in jeopardy and that my wife wanted a divorce. The prospect of losing your vision and having your marriage come apart is a brutal combination. I would not wish it upon anyone.

Regarding vision, I remember watching the Emilio Estevez-directed movie The Walk, in which Martin Sheen played an eye doctor. While golfing with doctors in other specialties, they give him grief for being just an eye doctor. Their insinuation is that what he does is not as important as what they do in the medical field. He simply stops playing golf and says, "The eyes are the most important organ in the body."

I had gone to the eye doctor because I thought my left eye needed a stronger contact. It seemed blurry. After a short exam, the eye doctor went to get a specialist. He came back and quickly diagnosed glaucoma and cataracts. As mentioned, I was just past my mid-40s at the time. The doctor said this is something that usually affects much older people. I was stunned. The next thing I knew, I was being slid into a tube at a hospital the next day to see if it was due to something terrible and life threatening in my head. I had to wait until the next day to see if I had a tumor or something in my head. It turned out that it was not a tumor, but the glaucoma was aggressive. It was tearing through my left eye like Sherman through Georgia in the Civil War. Thus began many trips to various eye specialists and eye surgeries.

While she was very supportive of my health challenge, about a year later my wife said she wanted a divorce. I won't get into all of the reasons because she is a dedicated mother, a professional at work, and a community volunteer—and we get along fine today—but the divorce and the glaucoma crushed me like nothing in my almost-fifty years of life at the time. I remember that, when it came time to move out of the home we had been in for ten years, I knew of a friend who had a rental home. I told her that I would take it sight unseen. I had no drive to go looking for a new place to live.

There were many days after that where a day of accomplishment for me was taking a shower. It was like getting knocked out by Mike Tyson in his prime. I had always been resilient and positive, but this was a whole new world. I went through a stretch where it was "one thing after another," as my Uncle Everett would say. In a gesture of kindness, I was offered the opportunity to go on a motor coach trip to Wrigley Field to see a Cubs game. Our group got there and my seat was right behind one of the huge beams in the stadium. Later, I was in Seattle and was given the number of a good restaurant to call. I dialed them up and the receptionist said, "You've reached rock bottom."

"You've got that right," I thought. It turns out that the name of the restaurant was "Rock Bottom." This time of my life was a mess. It made me think of the old song on the show "Hee Haw": "Gloom, despair, agony on me. Deep, dark depression, excessive misery. If it weren't for bad luck, I'd have no luck at all. Gloom, despair and agony on me…." However, I often go to inspirational quotes or scriptures to help me keep a positive attitude, and the one that came to mind was that hitting rock bottom is an event, not an address. Reflect on lessons learned, put on your work clothes, and use that rock bottom as a spring board to achieve new heights!

Maybe there was symbolism in the eye challenges as one eye, my left, was bad, while my right was pretty good. I often thought of that as negative and positive, which is what attitude is all about. When these things happen, we often wonder what is going on but I remember driving and listening to a Christian radio station when a pastor came on and said life was not going to be all smooth sailing. He also said that, when things like cancer or what I had came along, it wasn't God making those things happen, but allowing them to happen. The pastor had cancer and said that just because he was a pastor didn't mean he had a "pass" on getting anything serious like that disease. I remember to this day that the other thing he said was about how in Heaven everything would be healed. As I mentioned in the Four Needs chapter in this book, that gave me strength.

Even though I was devastated and a "charred husk" as I called myself, there are certain things I did to stay strong and stay positive:

* I kept going to my Church and staying around the body of believers. I met with my pastor.
* I made it a point to get to the fitness center where I worked out almost every day.

* I stayed true to the things I write about in this book and my attitude seminars.
* I took life one day at a time.
* While I got awfully low, I refused to contemplate ending it all because I firmly believed that God could turn my mess into a message. My mother took her life when I was 18 and my dad battled depression for years, so I was dealt a challenging hand. No doubt, staying strong in my faith and staying very active in my church were huge reasons I was able to overcome those dark days where you consider taking your own life. While I admit those thoughts darted into my head, a major reason I would never do that is because of how much it would hurt those closest to me. I also remember reading in Brett Eastburn's remarkable book *I'm Not Missing Anything* that, when he was considering ending it all as a school-aged kid with all kinds of challenges in life, he thought of himself as a rubber ball. That ball was hurtling to the ground, but when it hit it was going to soar back up. That's what Brett did. He hit rock bottom, but blasted back up and is now one of the top motivational speakers and stand-up comedians in the U.S.

One of the things it seemed like God did for me during this stretch was to make sure I always had a motivational keynote or a seminar to deliver when I was struggling the most. I would get to those places and suddenly find the strength to deliver a rip-roaring message. It would always energize me. It was as if God had my schedule covered!

As the months went by, I continued to try to look

for the positive. I remember telling myself that going through this would help me relate better to others in my speaking and writing. So often we see these polished motivational speakers up on stage with their sharp outfits, excellent posture, and golden lives. There is nothing wrong with that, but it often makes it harder to relate. I knew that I would have a deeper connection with audiences—and that has proven to be true. I have noticed an authentic connection with audiences. They can see that I really believe the things I talk about and, having been around over half a century, I have the good and bad laps on me to relate to them.

Another positive that came from all of this was that I had moved into a simple, small rental house in what appeared to be a "questionable" part of town. I had gone from a large home to one so small that a double bed would fit in only one of the bedrooms and it took up the whole room! Yet what happened over time was that I came to appreciate every little thing about that house. I found myself being grateful for a roof, warmth in winter, and a home, period. One thing I have always done is think of what the Apostle Paul wrote about learning to be content in all situations. If you can do that, it's huge in keeping a positive attitude. I found my neighbors to be good, hard-working people. One of my neighbors was a lady in her 80s with a big boat of a car that had all kinds of dents in it. We were outside talking one day when she said she had been hit by another car. She had all kinds of tape on that corner of the car. She said insurance didn't cover it. "Ah," she said, "what the heck. How often do I look at that corner of the car? The thing gets me around town. That's what matters!" She laughed. She wasn't settling. She just wasn't getting worked up about the whole thing.

One of the things I did—and I know a lot of people do this to stay positive as you also will discover as you read through this book—is to always realize that someone else has it tougher than me. You don't take the approach of being "happy" that they have a rougher "go of it" than you do, but it helps to put things in perspective. I happened to come across a review of Amy Ryan's book entitled *Shot: Staying Alive with Diabetes.* The attorney learned she had Type 1 diabetes at age 29. I read a *USA Today* article on her and one part really jumped out at me. It was when she shared this:

> Without a doubt, the hardest thing for me about living with type 1 diabetes is that you never, ever get a break from it. It requires attention, monitoring and adjustment every few hours—morning, noon, night and other times in between. Of course there are physical aspects of the disease that are tough—multiple glucose tests every day (I average about 10 a day), injections of insulin or infusion from insulin pumps, urine testing. But for me, it's never getting to take a day off that's the hardest. Emotionally, it's a demanding and exhausting disease."
>
> – Amy Ryan, from her book
> *Shot: Staying Alive with Diabetes*
> (Hudson Whitman/Excelsior College Press)

One of the wisest things I did during this incredibly hard time in my life was to seek help. I went to a man named Herman in my church after hearing him give a sermon on healing during difficult times. I asked if he would get a group together to pray with me. I told him about what I was going through. Herman got two other church members, Carol and Brian, and every Thursday I went to the church and they prayed over me. It was very humbling to go to a small room and get down on my knees but, when they rested their hands on me and prayed over me, it helped so much. I also opened up to them. I admitted to them that I had started drinking too much. With their help, I cut back dramatically on how much I was "hitting the sauce," as they say. Before prayer each Thursday, we would sit and talk. I would candidly share where I was struggling and where things were getting better. Their love and compassion was huge in helping me to get stronger by the week. I encourage you to reach out to your church or a local church. There are real people like Herman, Brian and Carol who will listen and pray with and for you. One of the things Herman helped me with was dealing with my vision challenges. He prayed that my eyes could be healed, but if that was not the case that I would have the strength to deal with the loss. From that, I came to tell God that His will be done with my eyes. It is awfully hard to start losing your vision after you have had 45 years of corrected 20-20 vision. Had I not had the counseling of Herman, Brian and Carol, I probably would have gone off the deep end. Through their help and prayers, I was able to quit drinking. That was something that had to be done. During my rough time, I slowly began drinking more and more and it was starting to get out of control. By opening up to them candidly about how bad it had become, I was able to take the steps to eliminate it and have been so much better off ever since.

I wanted to share a few things that also happened in my life that led me to quit drinking. Before I write about them, I want to say that I am not all "judgmental" towards anyone who drinks. There are plenty of folks who are reasonable drinkers. In my case, I was not and I had to do something about me.

I believe that God laid a few things on my heart over a stretch of about a year that led to my quitting. The first thing was that I learned that Chris Herren was going to share his riveting story of how he had become a professional basketball player, but threw his career away because of his addiction to drugs and alcohol. His presentation was going to be given at Benedictine University, two hours from my home. Despite the distance, I made the drive and was blown away by the power of his talk. Chris had been so talented at basketball that, while playing for Fresno State in college, he once scored 29 points against a Duke University team that was loaded with future NBA players. However, in college Chris began an addiction to drugs and alcohol that would reach unheard-of levels. He was so addicted to OxyContin that, while playing for the Boston Celtics, he had an experience that caused the audience listening to him at Benedictine University to gasp. He had put a call into his dealer to get more OxyContin the day of a Celtics home game. This is a man who grew up in Massachusetts and was able to play for the Celtics, but all that mattered to him was getting more drugs. During warm-ups before a home game, he kept going back to the locker room to check his phone to get the latest update from his dealer. While in there, the dealer called and said he was stuck in traffic near the Celtics basketball arena. Chris was so addicted that he ran out of the arena in full Celtics warm-up attire and down through the streets to meet the dealer. As he ran, a fan said, "Hey, that's Chris Herren!"

Chris reached low after low, but he said he finally fell to his knees and reached out to God and that began a recovery process that saw him become sober. That story and his whole one-hour talk resonated with me and planted a seed.

Not long after that, I hosted an Edgerton's group travel trip to Ireland. While there, I was reminded of a man I used to work with named Tom Csiszar, who was a very talented video cameraman in TV News. Tom and I worked together at WSBT-TV in South Bend, covering many Notre Dame football games. Back in those days, Tom was a heavy drinker. I can remember nights when we would be in Miami reporting on the Irish and would have an 8 a.m. news conference to cover the next morning. Tom would hit the whiskey hard, and it was all he could do to get the camera equipment to that news conference the next morning. The heavy drinking was killing him, but he cleaned up through Alcoholics Anonymous and became sober. I never will forget when WSBT sent Tom and me to Dublin in 1996 to cover the Irish as Notre Dame was over there for a few days to play Navy. Ireland is known for drinking, so I worried that the sober Tom might be challenged there. Not so! When we arrived, the first thing he did was go to an Alcoholics Anonymous meeting that night in downtown Dublin. He came back to the room beaming with a coin they had given him. While in Ireland in 2012 hosting that group travel trip, I thought of Tom often and thought that, if he could quit, then I could find the strength to quit too.

In addition, I recently went to see the movie *Flight* starring Denzel Washington as an airline pilot named Whip Whitaker, who had a huge drinking problem. He often drank and did drugs before flying but, because of his immense talent as a pilot, he was able to cover it up. I watched his character try to quit but then start again. One time he cleaned out all the liquor from his house. I related to that because I have been there and done that too. He kept relapsing and finally ended up in prison on a minimum 5-year sentence for flying a jet "under the influence" with over 100 passengers on board. The movie ended with his character in a support session with fellow inmates where he shares that he is happy being sober and that this makes him finally feel free. The final scene is of his estranged teenage son arriving at the jail to interview him for a school project. He asks his dad, "Who are you?" It's pretty obvious that he is in a much better place in his life.

Not too long after that I was in the grocery store. I never buy copies of *People* magazine, but I look at the pictures like a lot of other folks do while waiting to get to the register. But on this particular day, I think God put it on my heart to buy the issue with country singer Tim McGraw on the cover. I did and took it home and read it. McGraw shared how his drinking had been getting out of control over the years and was affecting his marriage. He candidly shared how he used to drink pretty heavily before concerts and how he had developed a beer gut. Five years before this article came out, he had quit drinking and has been sober ever since. He had also embraced a vigorous exercise program and, at age 45, had six-pack abs and was in awesome shape.

I like to pick up the *USA Today* newspaper from time to time, so later that day I popped into a minimart and got one. Guess who was the big feature story in their Life section? Tim McGraw, talking about quitting drinking and embracing exercise and much better eating habits. I truly believe God wanted me to read that, quit drinking, and take exercise and diet to another level. I may not be famous like Tim McGraw, but as a speaker in tip-top shape in his 50s, I can inspire others to make better choices regarding fitness and nutrition. I believe God was telling me that our bodies are temples and that we have to take better care of them. So, I went home, tossed out the sauce, and started working out like crazy. As I mentioned in Chapter 14, it was amazing how fast I became cut—even at age 50—when I was no longer dealing with all the empty calories of alcohol.

As I reflect now, many of the negative choices I made in life were a result of being influenced by alcohol. By giving it up, my positive attitude became stronger. Again, I never judge anyone on whether they drink or not, but I wanted to get personal in this chapter and share my story in hopes that it could help you in some way.

One thing that this brutal stretch of my life helped me to do was to relate better to people who have been beaten down in life. We often encourage people to "be positive" and "bounce back," but sometimes you get knocked on your ass and it isn't that easy. I could see why some people basically give up, especially those who have tried hard only to get blasted. After awhile you get to the point where you either barely care or you think more bad things will happen. I know because I wrestled with that for a time. I went through a phase where I felt I had tried really hard to do the right things, but had ended up getting smashed. "Why should I keep trying?" I said to myself, but by doing the things I write about in this book—staying connected to my church, and continuing to exercise—I slowly made it through.

That's why it is so important for us to encourage others and to dedicate the time to volunteer at community agencies that help people who are down and out. In his book *The Four Signs of a Dynamic Catholic*, Matthew Kelly writes: "The happiest people I know are also the most generous people I know. Is that a coincidence? I don't think so. The world proposes selfishness as the path to happiness. God proposes generosity as the path to happiness." I think Kelly nails it there. When you are generous with your time and your money, you become happier and you help those who are knocked down.

As I was going through this, I felt God encouraging

me to focus my motivational speaking on attitude and to write this book. My life experiences and especially that brutal stretch of my life definitely qualified me to help others to be as positive as possible. Since the challenges, I have had audience members and those who read my books and newsletters say that I have helped them in powerful ways. Another positive that came out of it was that I felt led to begin life coaching—and I love doing that now. I can relate to the challenges they have in their lives.

I hope this chapter has helped you. We all have had our rough stretches and maybe a stretch or two that just about leveled us but, if we take it one day at a time through that stretch, seek help, stay strong in our faith, and stay as positive as possible...we can do it!

—26—

The Amazing Attitude of Chandler McBride

IF YOU DOVE INTO A POOL and found yourself paralyzed, would you find the positive every step of the way from that point forward? Young Chandler McBride has taken that approach.

One of the things I do to stay positive is look for feature stories on inspiring people. That could be online, in a newspaper I pick up, or through DVD documentaries. While writing this book, I picked up my local newspaper and leafed through it to the Local section. While people say the media just reports negative stories, you can find positive features if you dig. Keeping a positive attitude takes work, which can mean digging in a negative world. I came across an Associated Press article that not only inspired me but stoked the fire within my attitude. There is a 17-year-old young man living in Michigan named Chandler McBride who has an attitude we all can learn from.

Chandler was paralyzed from the waist down after

a summer diving accident that happened just before his senior season. A talented high school athlete, he went from being a star on the football field to almost drowning in the pool after his accident. From the second the accident happened, he has made the choice to emphasize the positive. He told the Associated Press that he was thankful there was someone there to jump in and keep him from drowning. He said he was grateful for the doctors and nurses who treated him for 3½ months and for the friends who slept on his hospital room floor.

What really got to me in the article was when he said how thankful he was for his mother, Monica. She is single and has multiple sclerosis. Still, she gets up several times each night to turn her son so that he does not get bed sores. When I read things like that, it puts my challenges in life in perspective. What a special woman!

We hear so much that is negative these days that learning of stories like this reminds us that there are so many people doing positive things. The people in their community saw that Chandler would have to come back to a small two-bedroom apartment that would be hard to get around in a wheelchair. Contractors got a foreclosed home, gutted it and fixed it up for the family at no cost to them. Hundreds of people in the community pitched in and helped with interior designing, wiring, you name it.

These are the companies and groups that donated time, materials, services, and/or employees so that the McBrides were taken care of: Huddleston Lumber,

Marshall Trusses, Universal Forest Products, Graber Excavating, Sauber & Sons, Going Green Recycling, Richmond Sanitation, Lowes, Statler Flooring and Cabinets, Sherwin-Williams, Bogen Cement, Safety Glasses USA, Joe's Concrete, Jeff Todd Concrete, BTR Construction, Bel Aire Heating and Cooling, Rich Wheat Elec., Curtis Electric, Waste Management, Jeff Lind, McBride Drywall, Scott Outman, Sanderson Insulation, Scott Roderick Plumbing, Ray Friel, John Ambrosen, Woody Thompson Roofing, JD Construction, Midwest Energy Employees, G.W. Jones Bank, Southern Michigan Bank, Armstrongs, Kendall Electric, Forest River, and Homemakers Drywall.

Most of us don't know any of those businesses. The reason I listed them was to show what can happen when a community comes together.

The Associated Press story said that University of Michigan head football coach Brady Hoke and the Wolverines star player at the time, Desmond Robinson, had visited Chandler in the hospital and shared these words: "Don't give up. Fight like a champion." Ironically, Chandler had gone with his church youth group to hear a motivational speaker the day before his accident. The speaker had encouraged the audience to not look horizontally but to look vertically, to look up to God. At that conference Chandler bought a pendant that has the Bible verse from Joshua 1:9: "Be strong and courageous. Do not be terrified. Do not be discouraged. For the Lord your God will be with you wherever you go." He has held onto it tightly ever since the accident.

Later that fall Chandler was back on the high school football field in his wheelchair where he was pushed onto the field with his team. He returned to school with the goal of going to college to study neurology.

His attitude about his future is positive. He will not verbally or internally say that he is a paraplegic. He will not buy into the logic that he will never play again. Much of that attitude comes from having played sports. That taught him not to quit. The way he looks at it is that he is simply out of action right now. His positive mindset is that there will be a time when there will be a medical advance and the feeling will come back.

One of the ways I stay positive is by following stories like Chandler's. I "Liked" the Chandler McBride Facebook page. I checked it regularly. A story by the *Detroit Free Press* did wonders for my attitude. It was about how the Detroit Lions senior VP of Communications, Bill Keenist, had learned about Chandler when he was in a nearby hospital and went to visit him. Keenist was touched by Chandler's upbeat and positive attitude. Keenist told the *Free Press* that his life was "profoundly better" since he met Chandler and his mother, Monica. Keenist and the Lions arranged for Chandler to spend a weekend with the team and at their final home game of the season. At a practice, he was brought out on the field where he lined up in the offensive backfield. Star quarterback Matthew Stafford, with NFL superstar receiver Calvin Johnson lined up along with the rest of the Lions offense and defense, handed him the ball and Chandler wheeled into the end zone for a touchdown!

Chandler and his mom are making this experience as positive as possible. They are educating families on how to dive into pools and how to sled in the winter, so that they won't face the challenges that he is facing in life.

Positive things happen to positive thinkers. What a story! I think it was the end of the article that really got me. It simply concludes with him saying, "I will be thankful forever."

— 27 —

Don't Give Up!

WHEN A LOT OF NEGATIVE THINGS happen in life, it's human nature to consider quitting. After awhile you could go, "Enough!"

Here is an amazing story that can show you how sticking with it and staying as positive as possible can lead to amazing things in life. In 1992, the NorthWood High football program lost their beloved head coach Jim Andrews in a car accident. His assistant Rich Dodson took over amidst tremendous grief. Over time, NorthWood made it to the state championship game six times. They lost all six games. Their 2005 season started with their main quarterback not returning because of a disagreement. Their best 12th-grade athlete was lost for the year in the first game. They lost four of their first five games. They went to a 9th-grade quarterback who originally was supposed to be their third-string quarterback. You would think this team was like the *Titanic* heading towards an iceberg. This bunch looked like they would be the first football team at NorthWood

High to have a losing record in 34 years! But something very important happened to reinforce their positive attitude. When the players went home, they heard positive things from their parents. They told them to keep listening to their coaches and to stick together. Good things would happen.

Positive feedback! They got positive reinforcement, whereas in many cases today parents would want the scalp of the coach!

NorthWood finished the regular season with a 3-6 record. At the end of the regular season they were coming together as a team. The state football tournament in Indiana is set up where every team is in it regardless of their regular-season record, so NorthWood had a clean slate. Sometimes in life we just have to wipe away the past and say: "Tomorrow it all starts anew!"

Fueled with a positive attitude, the Panthers got on a roll. They won five straight games in the state tournament to reach the state title game in Indianapolis. Their opponent would be mighty Chatard High, a team that had defeated them in two previous title game encounters by a combined score of 72-6.

Amazingly, NorthWood beat them 7-0 for the state championship! It was the first time Chatard had been shut out in seventy-two games! The NorthWood team had not held a team scoreless all season until the state title game. NorthWood became the first team in Indiana history to win the state championship with six losses. Before then, only one of the 138 previous champions had even as many as five losses!

Their coach, Rich Dodson, summed it up this way: "You can't play like a champion until you think like one." Any team will face adversity. The real champions are the ones who pick themselves up, stay optimistic and figure out a way to get the job done. We never gave up. We competed in every game, even all of those that we lost. We always played with the attitude and the poise of a champion. This team won because it picked itself off the ground and blocked out the negativity. With anything in life that you try to do, that's the way to be a winner."

When you analyze what he said, there are so many things that apply to us whether we are in sports or not. He said you can't play like a champion until you think like one. He talked about staying optimistic and being solution-centered (figuring out a way to get the job done). Powerful stuff! He said their team did not have a single major college or potential Division-I college player. It was a case of their attitude becoming more positive once they got on a roll in the state tournament.

You may be facing adversity but, like the North-Wood Panthers, keep competing in the game of life! Go into each day, each situation, with the attitude of a champion!

When I speak, one of my points is about boxing. It has been said that rarely do boxers truly get knocked out. They just don't get up.

When they truly get knocked out is when they take a big blow and become unconscious and sent into next week. What usually happens, though, is they get hit hard and go to the mat, and just don't get back up. In life, we have moments like that where something hits us hard. It could be a breakup, a financial setback, a major disappointment, and it knocks us down like a punch from a heavyweight boxer in his prime. In boxing, a fighter can be down for several seconds. They just have to get back up before the referee counts to ten. You will have situations in life where you are down, but slowly get back up on one knee and then reach for the ropes (which in life could be someone to help), and bring yourself back up to both feet. Don't quit!

When have you been knocked down in life and thought of quitting?

____

____

____

____

____

____

What are you going to do about it?

____

____

____

____

____

____

____

____

____

—28—

"I Blame Jeff's Cancer"

JEFF LAFFERTY IS TAKING an on-fire, positive attitude towards the chronic lymphocytic leukemia he was diagnosed with in 2005.

Ironically, it is Lance Armstrong's foundation that has helped him from the start.

"When I first got cancer," Jeff told me, "the Livestrong people really helped me a lot. When you first get cancer you are so uncertain how it will affect you, your wife, your family. They had a person that calmly answered all of my questions and my wife's questions. They put us at ease."

The 41-year-old is on fire about battling it. "It can define you or I can define it," he said. "I have drawn a lot of inspiration from the Jim Valvano speech. I am defining it."

In 1993, the dying former college basketball coach gave an unforgettable talk that included these words: "Cancer can take away all of my physical abilities. It cannot touch my mind, it cannot touch my heart, and it cannot touch my soul."

I asked Jeff about his approach to attitude.

"I have always had a positive and glass-half-full attitude," he said. "I learned so much from growing up playing hockey. It taught me that, when something goes bad, you can't stay down or upset because you lose focus on the next thing coming up—and it could be something great. I always look through the front windshield rather than the rearview mirror. Another approach I have is not to get too high when things are going well and not to get too down when they are going the wrong way. It is never as bad as it seems and it is never as good."

Jeff, who is married with three children, ages 18, 13 and 10, has formed a popular Facebook group called Blame Jeff Lafferty's Cancer. "My friends will go on the page and blame my cancer for the small stresses that can occur in life," said Jeff, "anything from global warming to burnt and undercooked food. It was my way of telling my friends that it's okay and to turn a negative and have some fun with it and embrace it."

Here are some examples:

I blame your cancer for my grilled cheese not turning out right yesterday!

I blame Jeff Lafferty's cancer for my dog crapping in my truck this morning...damn cancer!

I blame Jeff's DAMN cancer for my engineering department being WOEFULLY understaffed AND we can't find qualified people who are willing to work CRAZY STUPID hours.

Jeff writes quite bit on the group page, often blasting the cancer. For example, when he has the strength to watch his daughter's recital, he lets the cancer know it! Here is something he wrote to vent:

Cancer...I am blaming you that I was so weak during my Relay for Life speech that I lost my spot and had to recover and end the speech but I was told that people were moved to tears with my speech. So, for that cancer... {{{{sticking tongue out}}}}

Jeff says people have been able to write emotional feelings about cancer in this group where they would feel a little uncomfortable sharing on their own Facebook wall. He says it also lets people know that he is okay about talking about it because a lot of people wonder whether or not someone battling cancer wants to discuss it.

"It's my kind of humor," Jeff said. "A lot of friends call me inspirational. I am humble. I do what I do. I don't get up in the morning and say I will inspire people."

Here is one of his posts:

I have my two hospital eight hours worth of chemotherapy to end this twice a day trips to st. joe medical center for chemotherapy...and also...ha ha ha...you couldn't keep me from being at the rink yesterday for my son's hockey game...so choke on that, cancer!

Jeff Lafferty is using his fire within and a positive attitude to take dead aim on cancer. He is truly an inspiration.

—29—

Strive to Be Solution Centered

TO BUILD AND KEEP that darn positive attitude, it is very helpful to be solution-centered as an individual and as an organization.

I had a human resources director come up to me after I had delivered my attitude program for their company and share her insights on this topic. She said she had a thick black line at her H.R. door. If someone came to her office griping about something, they had to have at least one solution before crossing that line. They usually showed up just to bellyache. They just wanted to storm in and rip on someone else or on a company policy. She would make them have at least one solution, so they often had to stand there a few minutes before coming inside. When they shared a solution, she had top quality chocolates to share with them. If anything, it took the edge off their negative vibe.

There was a college that had a problem with many of the students drinking heavily on Thursday nights. They changed it to where certain required classes were offered only at 8 a.m. on Friday's. That cut down on the Thursday night party central thing. As a former broadcaster, I used to cover the Daytona 500. It is now a huge event, but years ago it was small and held on the Daytona beaches. Rather than go through the ticket area, many fans would walk right through the nearby beach bushes and go in for free. The solution there was to put up signs that read "Beware of Snakes." I don't think snakes even mess with sand, but it worked. I once heard that in the olden days they had a problem with ants getting up in beds. The solution was to put the bed posts in aluminum cans filled partially with water. No more ants in the bed.

In China, a bus company wanted to make sure all their drivers were driving safely so they came up with hanging these huge, wide bowls of water next to the drivers. Those made the drivers navigate gently rather than zipping around like Jimmie Johnson. Video cameras were up above to capture any driver who spilled the water and tried to refill it.

There was a talented high school football player who was recruited by many schools, including rivals Auburn and Alabama. He initially picked Auburn and even got an Auburn tattoo. Then, he changed his mind and decided to sign with Alabama! The initial negative reaction could be to go, "Oh, no, what does he do with the tattoo? Does he get it removed, which can be painful?" Fans started coming up with solutions. Rather than remove the word "Auburn" why not add "Beat" in front of it so that it would read "Beat Auburn"? Or, the word "stinks!" could be added after it, since he would be playing for Alabama. I thought those were good solutions because our initial reaction would be that having it removed was the only solution.

To build and keep a positive attitude as an organization, it is important to nip in the bud the ol' "*They* should this" or "*They* should that" challenge. You can go almost anywhere and hear someone moan and complain about how "they" should do things. In every job interview and every training session, I would suggest addressing this issue because it is huge. It is so easy to pull out the "they" nonsense.

Here is a powerful personal example of how you can take a big-time challenge and turn it into a positive. During my television news years one of my biggest responsibilities was coordinating the coverage of Friday night high school basketball and football. Tens of thousands of potential customers would tune in for those 11 p.m. newscasts. Companies loved to advertise on them because of all the mothers, fathers, grandparents, aunts, uncles and everyone else that would watch. The usual drill was to have six video camera people go all over the viewing area to get eighteen games or so for the newscast. One year we had major challenges at the station, and I was told I was being cut back from having six to just three video camera people.

A fifty percent cut?! Whoa! I immediately could have launched into "they can't do this to us" and all that negative stuff, but I looked at it from the solution-centered approach right away. If you are in a leadership position, that is vital. Sure, inside I stewed a bit and was a little discouraged, but I quickly called for a meeting of the people we had and asked for solutions. We met for almost an hour and threw out all kinds of scenarios. As a team, this is what we came up with to deal with this large cutback: Instead of covering eighteen games, we would have one camera person cover three, another cover three, and the third one would cover...one! What?! Wouldn't you want to get as many games as you can? In our case what we decided to do was pick a big game of the week that would draw a lot of interest. We would then reach out to the coaches and ask for permission to videotape their pre-game and halftime talks to their teams. The camera person would shoot video of the game and then hustle back and put together a behind-the-scenes look at it. As it turned out, we would have one coach who would play opera music in the locker room before the game while the opposing coach would be wound up and stomping around the room writing all kinds of things on the chalkboard. Every coach had a different style and they were all interesting. Some were cool and calm. Others had veins bulging in their necks. It turned out to be a fascinating look at games. It drew in viewers that weren't interested in seeing a bunch of high school games. The ratings for the show went up and it was the talk of the town.

This was *after* a fifty percent reduction!

We did this for a couple of years until we got back to full strength with six camera folks, and kept it in the show in a shorter form. Eventually it ran its course and we stopped it, but to this day I believe it was a valuable example of being solution centered.

The more I was in the corporate world (and television news is the corporate world, big time), the more I became almost consumed with being solution centered. As an anchor, I would always go on the set a few minutes before my on-air appearance, put the microphone on my tie, and wait for the floor director to call for a microphone check. Sometimes that person would forget to do it. One time they came to me live after the commercial and the batteries in my microphone were dead. It sounded awful. To the viewers at home, I sounded like I was in a tin can and I had to clumsily put on a new microphone while live on the air. That destroyed the whole segment which had taken hours to produce. Rather than get negative, I immediately went into solution mode. From then on, every time I went onto the set, I put the microphone on and started saying, "Test, one, two three. Microphone check, one, two, three." I never had a mike go dead on me again.

Where in your life have you been more of a belly-acher and how can you be more solution centered?

____

____

____

____

____

____

____

—30—

Live Like 'Line

WHENEVER MY POSITIVE ATTITUDE takes a hit and is reeling, I often think of Caroline Found's mother somehow finding the strength to walk through their church.

One October evening I was moved to tears by one of the most inspirational stories I have ever seen. I was in my hotel room when a promo for Bryant Gumbel's Real Sports show on HBO came up and told of a very inspirational story that had to do with a girl named Caroline in Iowa. I realized that if the story had made it to the national stage of a "60 Minutes"-type show like that, it had to be special.

Frank Deford is one of the most respected journalists ever. He had traveled to Iowa with a camera crew because of a letter written to him by a high school volleyball coach who wanted to share the story of Caroline and her mother, and felt no one could do it better than Deford. The letter so touched Deford that he said to himself that he had to do the story.

Caroline Found was a 12th-grade volleyball player for West High in Iowa City. She was a setter, the most important position on the court, and one of the best players in the state. She had led her team to the state title as an 11th grader. Deford's feature showed her great passion for life as she led her team in upbeat and often funny warm-up drills. You could tell she was a great kid with a huge heart. Every picture of her showed the zest for life she had and the positive attitude she carried into every day.

You could also tell her friends adored her. The only thing that seemed to affect her attitude was her name Caroline. She insisted her friends call her " 'Line." The daughter of a doctor and a mother who was a hand therapist, her life was ideal until out of nowhere her mother, Ellyn, was told she had stage 4 pancreatic cancer. In her early 50s, she had weeks to live.

As I was watching the story, I thought it was heading in the direction that young Caroline would dedicate the season to her mother and lead her rebuilding team to yet another championship.

Not this story.

Caroline, 17, was leaving a church youth function on her moped to drive to the hospital to spend the night with her mom, who was within a week or maybe a little more from dying. Caroline lost control of the moped after it hit a curb and she went into a tree where she died instantly.

When that part of the story was told, I almost could not grasp that it had happened.

The news devastated the community. Her friends

literally threw themselves to the ground with overwhelming grief and shock. The father, Ernie, had to gather the strength to go to the hospital to tell Ellyn that her daughter had died. Ernie said his wife was on medications to help her handle the pain of the cancer and that made it harder for her to grasp what had happened, but she did.

Thousands of people from all over Iowa came to pay their respects at the visitation and services. Entire volleyball teams drove hours to stand in line for up to four hours to honor Caroline's memory. The video in the story that will stay with me forever was of the church service. They had to get a special medical vehicle to drive Ellyn to the service, and once there, they helped her into a wheelchair where her cancer-ravaged body was taken to sit near the casket. At the end of the service, Deford reported that, as they started to wheel Ellyn out and back to the hospital, she told them she wanted to walk back down the aisle to the church door.

In a video that was shot from up above in the church, Ellyn can be seen gingerly taking small steps, moving her way up through the main aisle. As she is going, she places her hands on the shoulders of mourners and gives them the warmest smile I have ever seen. It is as if she is thanking them for being there.

As one who has put together thousands of features and stories during my TV-News days, I can't ever remember seeing a more inspirational segment of video. The way she put her frail hand on shoulders and the smile she gave them was as if she was more concerned that they were okay.

That funeral was on August 16th. Ellyn went back to the hospital where she died one week later on August 23rd. Caroline had died August 11th. As sad as it was, life moved on and the volleyball team had to go into the season without their best player. They already had to replace a lot of players from the championship team of the previous year, leading their coach to say she expected them to be awful.

To honor her, the players decided to approach the season and life with the motto: "Live like 'Line." One of Caroline's best friends reluctantly took the position of setter. She struggled mightily at the start of the season, and the team did not do well. The coach, Kathy Bresnahan, was having a very hard time missing Caroline as a person and cried out to her one day to please send a sign she was okay. The coach said that shortly after that she started finding pennies in sets of three in all kinds of different locations.

The team got to the state tournament and got it rolling. They won one match, then another, and another and made it to the state championships. In a best-of-5 match, their team lost the first two sets. They battled back and won the next two and, despite trailing 14-13 on match point, they dug down deep and won!

They celebrated on the court for the longest time. The coach went up into the stands and hugged Ernie for the longest time. He had watched the championship match while holding a framed picture of Caroline. The coach took it back down on the court to be with the players, and one of the final scenes of the story shows the fans and players singing Neil Diamond's "Sweet Caroline." The players would say "Sweeeeet Caroline" and the fans would go "whoa, whoa, whoa!"

The school and community continue to approach each day with the "Live like 'Line" attitude of being positive, caring for others, and looking for the good in others. When it comes to staying positive and being on fire, the story of Caroline Found and the incredible strength of her mother in that church are powerful examples that we can all draw from in life. I know if I find myself discouraged about something, I will think of Caroline's mother walking up the main aisle of that church encouraging others.

—31—

Half-Empty or Half-Full?

LET'S SAY YOU GET HOME and suddenly realize your favorite television show is on at that moment. You forgot to record it. You frantically turn on the set and see that it is halfway over. Are you grateful that you get to see the remaining fifteen minutes or all bent out of shape that you missed the first fifteen minutes?

NEGATIVE PERSON RESPONSE: "!%#@*! I forgot to record it!! Why even watch the last part?!"

POSITIVE PERSON RESPONSE: "Oh, man, I missed the first half. Next time I will put it in my calendar to make sure it's recorded (solution centered right away). Alright, now I will sit down and see how it ends. I have watched this sitcom enough to where I can get up to speed on what the plot is pretty quickly. Getting mad about missing the first part isn't going to help things..."

Your response says a lot about where you are with positive attitude. We all have heard about the glass being half-full or half-empty. One thing you can do each day at work or at home is put out a glass that is half full. Glance at it from time to time to build up that "half-full" attitude.

There were two farmers. One was very positive while the other was all negative. When it came time for the crops to grow, the negative farmer moaned about how they wouldn't get enough sun. The positive farmer reassured him that things would be okay. Sure enough, there was plenty of sun. Then that ol' negative farmer grumbled about how there wouldn't be enough rain or too much rain. Again, the positive farmer talked about good outcomes and the rain was fine. After awhile that positive farmer decided he needed to do something for his crotchety friend so he took him out duck hunting. They were out on the lake in the positive farmer's boat where they got a few ducks. The positive farmer smiled as he couldn't wait for what was next! "Watch this," he said to the negative farmer. "This is my new Labrador Retriever!" He then sent the dog off the side of the boat to get the ducks. The dog ran ON TOP of the water out and back! It was amazing. The positive farmer turned to the negative one excited for what had to be an upbeat response....

"Just like I thought," the negative farmer said with a surly look on his face. "Your dog can't swim...."

Now THAT'S a negative fellow! Hey, it is all about how we look at every situation in life, including challenges. There was a little boy who loved baseball. He had a dream of being a great hitter in the Major

Leagues. He went out behind his house one day with a bat and a ball and he tossed that ball up in front of himself with intentions of hitting it far! "I am the best hitter in baseball," he said as he took a mighty swing at the ball as it came back down. "Whoosh!" He missed the ball. Still optimistic, he picked it up and did it again. "I am the greatest batter there ever was!" he said as he swung so hard he lifted off the ground. "Whoosh!" He missed it again. This went on and on with him missing fifteen times.

On the fifteenth miss and for every one after that he said, "I'm the greatest PITCHER of all time!"

This youngster started out thinking hitting was his gift. It sounds like throwing the ball was his future. He looked at things differently.

What is something in your life you could look at from a different perspective?

—32—

Have an Attitude of Gratitude!

WHILE YOU CAN CERTAINLY study positive attitude and break it down into all sorts of compartments, it is also important to realize that it is basically a very simple but powerful concept. Many of my insights on positive attitude have come from having hosted dozens of Edgerton's group travel trips over the years. On many of the trips that utilized a motor coach, we had a driver named Gary Bays. Gary was always upbeat. The travelers loved him. Besides driving, he had funny jokes. He always had a funny hat to wear, depending on where we were on the trip. In Memphis he bought some big Elvis sunglasses to have when the travelers got back to the motor coach from visiting Graceland. At one point I went up to him and had this short conversation:

Charlie: "Gary, you are always positive. What is your approach there?"

Gary: "I just have an attitude of gratitude."

There it is. I could write 814 pages in this book and include seven CDs and three DVDs with my observations on positive attitude but, if you want to cut to the chase, then listen to Gary. If you have an attitude of gratitude each day, you have a tremendous foundation for your positive attitude.

Another friend sent me her thoughts along these same lines:

> Charlie, I KNOW it sounds corny (believe me—it sounds corny to me and I DO it), but try it for just one week and I think this one can single-handedly change your attitude. Forever. Live with a gratitude attitude! When your alarm clock rings, don't hit the snooze button—not even once. Throw back the blankets, swing your feet over the side of the bed and as they hit the floor say (aloud!), "Lord, let's make it a great day!" Also, get outside! Enjoy nature's beauty even for just 30 minutes a day. Take in the sky, the smells, the fresh air and, most important, the sunshine. If you can't get outside, throw open the curtains—or better yet, throw them away. Let the sunshine in...your home, your mind, your heart, your spirit and your soul.
>
> *– Jill Garris, Marketing/Group Sales in Tourism Industry*

I want to take it one more step. Having an attitude of gratitude doesn't mean that you accept everything in your life and go around being thankful for the way things are for you. In many areas, I feel you need to be grateful—but don't settle. For example, if a lady is in a relationship with someone who is clearly a negative force in her life, then it would be wrong to take the approach of "I'm grateful to have him and I should be thankful that I have someone while many others don't have anyone." No, if that person is damaging in whatever way, then move on from that negative. Don't settle.

If you have a job, then I understand it is an "attitude of gratitude" to be thankful that you have a job—but that doesn't mean you have to settle for it. Neither does it mean you have to chase some position that will bring more money but more headaches as far as extra stress, office politics and such. But on the other hand, don't ever stop growing. At the same time, as you do continue to grow, always keep that attitude of gratitude. It's like when I learned that I had glaucoma and cataracts in my eyes in my 40s. It led me to be grateful for how healthy I was otherwise in life and that my children have all been healthy. I spent time in reflection and became very grateful for so many other blessings in my life, but I didn't settle for the eye conditions. I have seen multiple doctors and had many exams and operations as I strive to make it better.

In summary, here is a suggestion on how to approach positive attitude:

* Have an attitude of gratitude;

* Still, don't settle.

Always be grateful but don't always accept things as they are in life. Having an attitude of gratitude doesn't mean you sit around all day saying, "Well, I will settle for things as they are and be grateful…"

Write down 10 things you are grateful for in your life:

____

____

____

____

____

____

____

____

____

Write down 3 things that you will not settle for as status quo:

____

____

____

Write down 5 people that you are grateful for in your life and make it a point to reach out to one via phone, letter, email or Facebook to thank them:

____

____

____

____

____

—33—

"Cancer, I Am Going to Kick Your A**!"

BECAUSE HER PARENTS had emphasized having a positive attitude while she was growing up, Lauri Roberts was well equipped when cancer came calling.

Lauri Roberts was 39 years old in August of 2007 when she was diagnosed with breast cancer. Four days before her diagnosis, her best friend, Renae Winzer Johnson, was told she had breast cancer. The breast cancer stoked the fire within Lauri and Renae. Renae's response was to get up each morning, walk in the bathroom, look in the mirror and say, "Cancer, I am going to kick your a**!"

Lauri went into the battle with both guns blazing too. Lauri stared the most intense chemos in the face and said, "Bring it on." On her 40th birthday, she took the last of what's called "the Red Devil," the biggest gun you can get in treatment. During all of this she rarely missed work at the Department of Economics and Policy Studies at Notre Dame.

"I had the best boss in the world," she said in talking about Jennifer Warlick. "She took the day off from work when I had my first eight-hour surgery," Lauri said. "She was there all day. Then, when I came back to work, she bought a memory foam cot so I could rest on it during lunch."

Because of her determination, the only time they had to hire a temp worker was during the days around her surgery time. During chemo and everything else, Lauri was back on the job. At lunch she would have soup and then nap.

Attitude is so critical, especially in today's world. Her parents, Gene and Judy Montgomery of Edwardsburg, Michigan, had emphasized positive attitude when they were raising her.

"My mother and father both preached 'negative breathes more negative,' " she said. "They always said you have to find something positive in everything. I owe much of my recovery, and almost all of my positive outlook to them."

I talked with Lauri's mother Judy about what it is like when your grown daughter is diagnosed with breast cancer. Her answer was quick. "I turned it over to the Lord," she said. Judy said she had a firm grip on what she could control and couldn't control. What she could control was taking care of her grandchildren and getting them to school.

"She also sent 'save the date' prayer cards with a little pink pin and included both our names and surgery dates, and sent pink socks to my girlfriends to wear," said Lauri. "She showed no chinks in the armor. No tears. It was 'Let's do this.' That was very helpful to me."

Things that she could control…

"I never saw either of my parents despair when they heard the news," said Lauri. "Their attitude was, 'A little challenge, but you will get through this, and we will help.' "

Her father, Gene, drove her to and from work every day for six months during chemo. From her home in Edwardsburg, Michigan, to Notre Dame was at least 30 minutes each way—more in the winter. "I treasure those times in the car, talking with my father," said Lauri. "I grew to love my mornings with him. I miss our coffee talk."

Positive experiences come out of negatives...

"My girlfriends hired a housecleaner for six months," she said. "People came out of the woodwork to help."

Lauri has battled hard, and her sun is shining brightly. "I have an excellent prognosis," she said.

"We didn't realize what we had before all of this," Lauri said of her husband Kelly and their two children. "This has made my family stronger. During all of it, my husband wrote something on the dry-erase board in our house. It was 'Find Something Happy in Every Day.' Something! And we did."

I caught up with Renae, a Channel Account Manager for Cisco Systems, in early 2013.

"Last October (2012)," she said, "marked my being cancer free for five years. In November of that year, I remembered an article I had read in college that had a quote along the lines of: 'Are you living your life goals or are you just living?' I had work goals but I didn't have that next big thing. I found a book I had read years ago about 1001 things to do before you die and one was to climb a mountain. So, I set my sights on Mt. Kilimanjaro."

Renae trained hard for over a year and tackled it in February of 2013. She has the "fire within" that I talk about in my keynote "Stoke the Fire Within."

"I love life," she told me. "Attitude is the most important thing. Every day is a chance to be happy or miserable. I am a strong believer in 'the more you put out there, the more you get in return.' One of the things I do to stay positive is I always have snapshots in my head of positive memories."

One of the things Renae has come to realize is that, even when you have it hard, someone else has it harder. "My co-worker was dealing with liver cancer when I had the breast cancer," she said. "I called him up and expected him to be so sympathetic. He was more challenging in that he said, 'This is your opportunity to show the world how positive you can be…be sure not to give them any opportunity to treat you differently. If you ever have a bad day, then call me.' "

I asked Renae what advice she would give those who are diagnosed with cancer. "It's not the cancer that kills you," she said, "but dealing with the hospitals and the appointments and everything. You need advocates to go with you and take notes. It is important to utilize your friends and family network! Ask yourself what is your goal. If it is to live, then do whatever it takes. Be very aggressive. Part of my success was that, if I had known all the stuff that was coming at me—divorce, my dad dying, my cancer—I don't know how I would have come out, but I just kept getting up every day and bobbing and weaving through the day, taking it one hour at a time."

"In many ways the cancer was a blessing," she said. "It was as if you were dead but alive to see. I saw how many people loved me. The company I work for [Cisco Systems] was amazing. I could take off as much as I wanted."

Renae and Lauri are two great examples of how "on fire" and positive attitudes can make a difference!

Renae put climbing a mountain on her bucket list. Write down five things on your bucket list:

____

____

____

____

____

____

____

____

____

____

—34—

The Most Positive Person You Know

WHO IS THE MOST POSITIVE PERSON you know? I bet it doesn't take long for an image to pop up in your head. There is usually someone in our family or that we work with who jumps out when it comes to positive attitude! In writing this book, I decided to reach out to those who follow my daily inspiration on attitude with the question: "Who is the most positive person in your life?" The answers below are treasure as they can help you build up your attitude to be even stronger:

"Charlie, it's my daughter Shayna. She was diagnosed with diabetes at age ten and with myasthenia gravis at fourteen, which is a muscle weakness disease. Shayna always stays upbeat and positive despite her many physical challenges. She inspires me every day! One thing Shayna does every day: she looks out for other people who have disabilities, or just look like they need a friend. She makes a special point to go up to them and say hello, or just make sure they feel included in some way—like an offer to sit at the cafeteria lunch table. Shayna has been teased enough about her "droopy eye" that she is really more aware of those who are worse off. She also NEVER complains about her conditions...her attitude is that there is always someone worse off than her, and she needs to deal with the hand that God dealt her. I will never forget one day when she was in 7th grade. She was having episodes of muscle weakness that were causing her to fall at random. I didn't want her to go to school...because I was worried that she'd fall. Shayna just looked at me and said, 'Mom, don't worry! If I fall, I'll just get up again. That's what I do!' And that IS what she does, every day."

– Beth Erwin Davis

"My non-verbal autistic son, Christopher! He has accomplished so much more than was ever expected of him. He is my hero and a great role model for his little brothers!! He has a great attitude!"

– Kelly Grall Foster

"Charlie, the most positive person in my life has been my mother, who lost her battle with breast cancer eight years ago. She always had a wonderful attitude that we will never forget!!! That certainly impacted anyone who came into contact with her!!! During chemo, being very ill, never once did she have a negative thought or word. When we lost her, I made a promise to her and to myself to be that person. I always try to make good out of any situation. It has worked as I wake up every single day happy and with a positive attitude!!! I always remember there is always someone out there who has it much worse and a positive attitude makes for positive results!!!

"Her name was Judy Benn. [There are] two things that happened when she was ill that I will never forget and I always think of when it comes to attitude. She was at the oncologist's office and Dr. Zon told her that it had spread to her skull and three other places and there was nothing more they could do. Instead of my mother breaking down, she calmly says, 'Ok, well, I have three daughters…is there a test or something they can do to see if they have the breast cancer gene?' I was shocked that here she had a wonderful attitude, wasn't worried about dying, and was more worried about us!

"Then one other time in the hospital, it was just the two of us and she looked at me and said, 'Toni, I will not have enough time to find Todd (her husband) another woman before I die.' She just always thought of others first and always had such a positive outlook on life, even when she knew she was dying. It's really changed my life and I just try to live each day as she would have!!! Thank you, Charlie, for letting us share these stories in this book!"

– Toni Siomos Bailey

"Charlie, the person with the best attitude I have ever seen would be our mom. I think she got her great attitude from her mom who lived to be 100. Our mom passed away at 96—only four years ago—after having colon surgery. Prior to that, she had four bouts with cancer, with one removing her breast. She never questioned why her. She always felt someone else was worse off than she was and she made the best of a bad situation, whatever it might be. She had many, many friends and she would have given them anything they needed—and she did. We love and miss her bunches and I only hope that I am what she was to friends, family and anyone who crosses my path. Thanks to mom for being that great mom, grandma, great-grandma."

– Barb Blondell DeJarnatt

"Charlie, the best attitude I know of is that of my mom, Norma Switalski. Nothing stops her, despite being confined to a wheelchair. She is a huge fan of the local minor league baseball team and the local women's college basketball team. She gets to church by way of her wheelchair. She takes the city bus all over to get meds, food and necessities. She helps others and does many things for residents of her senior citizen building. You can find her out and about in downtown daily, living life to the fullest. A true example of what a positive attitude will get you!"

– Alice Switalski Vanmeter

Who is the most positive person in your life?

____

____

____

____

____

____

____

—35—

Scriptures to Help You Stay Positive

WHEN I DELIVER "How to Build a Positive Attitude and KEEP the Darn Thing!!" in seminar form, inevitably faith comes into play as to how very many people stay as positive as possible. I don't do it in a preachy way but, in my umpteen bazillion interviews with people over the years, many have cited how their faith foundation has been pivotal in their being content, upbeat, and positive.

> Charlie, my "life verse" is Philippians 4:13: "I can do all things through Christ which strengtheneth me" (King James version). During the 12 years I've battled multiple sclerosis, that verse has taken on as many new meanings as my disease has taken whacks at me. In the worst times, I'll tell God, "I can't," and He'll tell me, "We can."
>
> *– Mary Ellen Shedron, former journalist for Schurz Communications*

In church one Sunday my pastor, Dr. Pat Somers, shared how he utilizes sets of scriptures from the Bible to stay positive. He said the primary verses he goes to would be Philippians 4:4-9:

> Rejoice in the Lord always. Again I will say, rejoice! Let your gentleness be known to all men. The Lord is at hand. Be anxious for nothing, but in everything by prayer and supplication, with thanksgiving, let your requests be made known to God; and the peace of God, which surpasses all understanding, will guard your hearts and minds through Christ Jesus. Meditate on these Things. Finally, brethren, whatever things are true, whatever things are noble, whatever things are just, whatever things are pure, whatever things are lovely, whatever things are of good report, if there is any virtue and if there is anything praiseworthy—meditate on these things. The things which you learned and received and heard and saw in me, these do, and the God of peace will be with you.

Verse 6 reminds us to consider, what good does it do to worry or to be wound up about anything? Take it to God. Verses 8 to 9 really hit home in how important it is to focus on our thoughts and what we put into our head and hearts. It is impossible to think negative at the same time you are thinking positive; so if you have a group of positive things to go to in your thoughts, keep going to them until it becomes second nature.

Dr. Somers said that another verse he goes to is Psalm 118:24: "This is the day the Lord hath made; we will rejoice and be glad in it."

> God's word keeps me focused and positive. You know my obsessive-compulsive disorder gets the best of me and I find myself stressing over being the best even though I fail miserably on a daily basis. I meditate on

> Philippians 1:6—"Being confident of this very thing, that he which hath begun a good work in you will perform it until the day of Jesus Christ." What an amazing promise to cling to! Paul was such an encouragement to the early churches.
>
> – *Cindy DeMaso Beals*

Here are more scriptures to help you with your positive attitude:

"Therefore do not worry about tomorrow, for tomorrow will worry about its own things. Sufficient for the day is its own trouble." (Matthew 6:34)

As I focus on elsewhere in this book and my seminars, focus on today. That seems simple but so often our attitudes are damaged by moping over the past and fretting about the future.

"For I know the plans I have for you, declares the Lord, plans for welfare and not for evil, to give you a future and a hope." (Jeremiah 29:11)

"Keep your life free from love of money, and be content with what you have, for he has said, 'I will never leave you nor forsake you.' " (Hebrews 13:5)

There is nothing wrong with having money but the Bible clearly states to make sure you don't fall in love with it. When I was in television news I saw plenty of wealthy pro athletes and broadcasters who looked pretty miserable to me. Despite all that money, it often was never enough for them.

"Brothers, I do not consider that I have made it my own. But one thing I do: forgetting what lies behind and straining forward to what lies ahead, I press on toward the goal for the prize of the upward call of God in Christ Jesus." (Philippians 3:13-14)

To maintain a positive attitude we have to let go of the boneheaded things we have done in the past. It is important to change our ways if they have been wrong but, once you have made those changes, turn and face the future with the mindset of reaching that finish line of life in strong fashion!

"Rejoice always, pray without ceasing, give thanks in all circumstances; for this is the will of God in Christ Jesus for you. Do not quench the Spirit." (1 Thessalonians 5:16-19)

The most positive people are the ones who can find a way to have thankful hearts in ALL circumstances, not just when things are going well and they are "happy." Elsewhere in this book I share Sandra Herron's quote: "You can celebrate life or you can suffer life and it has absolutely nothing to do with your circumstances."

What is the Bible verse you will memorize and have as your "go to" scripture on attitude?

—36—

The Positive Attitude of Mike Edwards

IN MY BROADCASTING CAREER, I was fortunate to interview and get to know Mike Edwards, who has one of the most positive and on-fire attitudes I have ever seen. Mike was born missing a bone in his left leg. The leg didn't grow correctly, leaving amputation as the only option. A dedicated basketball player, Mike held off on the amputation. He would come home from practice and soak his leg in a bucket of ice to handle the brutal pain. While other kids were thinking about what game to play after school, young Mike was thinking about whether he would have to have his leg removed. Finally, it got to be too much. At age 13, he had the amputation and continued to play with an artificial leg.

Mike and his family moved to South Bend. He didn't tell anyone about his leg and earned a spot on the varsity team at John Adams High School based on his basketball skills. He wore sweats all the time to hide his artificial leg. Eventually, he had to take off the sweats. You can imagine how surprised his teammates were! They really didn't know how to act around him. There was a period of awkwardness.

Mike sensed it. Even though he was one of the most intense athletes to ever play at Adams High, he also knew when to loosen things up. As the team rode a bus across town to a scrimmage, Mike took off his artificial leg and held it out the window and waved it at passing cars. His teammates got the biggest charge out of that. Everyone laughed! Then, when they arrived at the opponent's school, Mike put the leg on backwards. With the other school's administrators waiting outside the bus to greet the visitors, Mike walked off with one foot heading forward and the other foot heading backwards. The administrators about hopped out of their pants!

Although Mike is one of the most intense, dedicated people I have ever met, he also knows when to have fun! He had the ability to laugh at himself, which is huge in staying positive. He wasn't making light of his own situation in a bad way. He was simply finding a way to use humor in his challenge.

His story attracted the interest of John MacLeod, who was then the Notre Dame head basketball coach. He invited Mike to be a walk-on for the Fighting Irish basketball team, where he would serve as a fierce practice player. I remember interviewing him before practice one time. His eyes were squinted just a bit as he told me he would do anything to help the team in practice. "I will sweat blood," he said. "Anything I can do to make these guys better!"

At the same time, he continued to find humor. He often joked that he was a 20/20 player for Notre Dame.

He would only get in a game if the team was up by 20 points or down by 20!

Mike went on to become the first disabled player in the history of Division I College Basketball to play in a game, when he got in a game November 8, 1998. Mike ran up the court, caught a pass, took two dribbles, and swished a shot. The crowd of 8,000 erupted.

The thing that I remember from interviewing and covering Mike was his perspective. While many thought he drew a tough lot in life, his visits to children in hospitals showed him there were many others who had it far worse then he did in life. I also remember being so impressed by his determination. He wanted to be an example to show people that, if you worked hard enough, stayed positive and kept a determined attitude, you could do just about anything you set your mind to!

—37—

A Threat or...Challenge?

SOME OF THE BEST LEADERS in America are the coaches of the athletic teams at small colleges such as Washington University in St. Louis, the University of Chicago, Tufts, Emory, Benedictine University, DePauw and Kenyon. They inspire and motivate athletes to championship levels at many of the top academic institutions in the land.

Many of these athletes from small college programs are coveted by companies because of the fire they bring to organizations. Their attitudes are always built on positive approaches to every situation.

Jim Steen was the swim coach at Kenyon College until he retired in 2012. Steen took over the Kenyon men's program and started the women's program in the 1975-76 season. Since then, he directed the Lords to 29 of their record 31 consecutive NCAA national championships and guided the Ladies to 21 of their 23 national titles. Steen has won more NCAA national championships (50) than any other coach in any NCAA sport.

Building and keeping a positive attitude mean knowing what to do when adversity or a challenging situation confronts you in life. One of his best swimmer's, Tracy Menzel, credits him for inspiring her to become a champion. She says there is one particular quote he says that really stands out: "You can approach anything two ways—under a threat or for the challenge."

Adversity can cause you to flinch or bear down. You can back down or burr up. To look at it as a challenge is to roll up your sleeves and know that positive results are headed your way. To look at it as a threat is to lean back on your heels and start thinking of the negative possibilities.

> Charlie, what I usually do...pray. And I can honestly say, over the last two decades of ups and downs in my professional life, every time I said, "O.K., God, this is Yours, work it out," He did. Seriously, every single time. Not once have I been let down by God. Not much magic in that method for someone who doesn't have faith at the center of their life but, boy, it sure works for me!
>
> *– Dan Tudor, Tudor Collegiate Strategies*

Back to Coach Steen. A *New York Times* article on him dug deep into why his teams are so successful. For decades he has instilled the philosophy to all his swimmers that everybody has a redeeming quality; as teammates, their job is to find the positive in one another and let go of the rest.

> Charlie, when I get down about something, I try to tell myself it could be worse, and I'm very blessed to have two healthy children who turned out to be awesome adults, and two healthy granddaughters that I get to spend a lot of time with—which I love!
>
> *– Patty Holston*

What is a situation in your life that you need to look at as a CHALLENGE?

____

____

____

____

____

____

____

____

____

— 38 —

If the Right Arm Doesn't Work...

THERE IS MORE NEGATIVE NEWS than ever before in the media. Obviously, these are challenging times, but tens of thousands of positive, upbeat things are happening every hour out there.

When I deliver "How to Build a Positive Attitude and KEEP the Darn Thing!!" to organizations, I talk about the importance of taking personal responsibility to make sure the fire within you is constantly stoked. If you don't, the negativity out there will snuff it out.

Let me share an example of "practicing what I preach," so to speak. I read in my local paper that the Rotary Club was going to honor disabled workers in my community. They had asked a man named Rick Melton to give the keynote. Rick is the head of the Art Department at LaVille High School. He is unable to walk without assistance and has limited use of the right side of his body.

I wrote down in my calendar that I needed to be there to hear his story. I called the phone number listed in the paper and found out the event would start at noon, be over about 12:50, and would cost $12—which would go to a local charity. I put it in my Planner.

On October 15th, I arrived at the South Bend Century Center a little before noon. Rick's amazing artwork was on display near the head table. The program started and, within thirty minutes, Rick was speaking. He said he had never given a speech before. He was nervous as he looked out over the large crowd that included the mayor of the city. As a professional speaker, I knew that, if he spoke from the heart and shared how he had stayed "on fire," he would be a knockout. Forget all that smooth, professional-posture stuff.

Back in 1985, Rick had just finished 9th grade when a semi forced the car he was in to go off the road. He suffered awful spinal cord injuries, causing the doctor to tell him he would never move again. He fought through the diagnosis with lengthy rehab and regained some motion. However, he had to teach himself how to use his left hand for art. He had always used his right, and it wouldn't move anymore. The following is what Rick told us about overcoming the massive challenges he faced in life:

> We all come across different obstacles in life. I had, and have, a strong faith in God. During rehab I prayed at night, thanking the Lord for the small gains I had made that day in rehabbing my body.
>
> My mother quit her job to help me. For her, failure was not an option. She kept me going. My father took it hardest. He is a good man, a hard worker. The medical bill was $150,000.

> Remember, this was back in 1985. I felt for my sister. She didn't get a lot of attention because so much was focused on me. I have a great family that sacrificed for me.
>
> I talked with a college counselor and said that, even in my physical condition, I wanted to take college prep courses in high school. The counselor said, "Why? Aren't you in a wheelchair? Don't you get a check from the government every month?!"
>
> You should have seen the look on my mother's face.
>
> After graduating from high school, I went to Indiana University — South Bend. After graduation from there, Goodwill helped me with job applications. For 150 days one year, I subbed in South Bend schools. I got a break and got a part-time teaching job at Marian High School. By my second year there, I was head of the Art Department. The principal at Marian went to LaVille and brought me there. I've been at LaVille High School nine years as Head of the Art Department. In 2002, Wal-Mart named me "Teacher of the Year."
>
> I've learned a bunch. It's a crazy world. Stuff happens. It doesn't make much sense, but you have to make the most of it.
>
> — *Rick Melton, Head of Art Department,*
> *LaVille High School*

Everyone in the audience gave Rick a standing ovation at the end of his first-ever speech. Everyone left inspired and determined to be as positive as possible. Our fire within had been stoked! How can you not be thankful and positive after hearing such a story?

This man is an inspiration to us all—especially his students. Remember, he had grown up using his right hand for his art. He had to totally re-teach himself to use his left hand. I can't even shave with my left hand.

By going to hear him talk, I was able to strengthen my positive attitude. I think of Rick's story from time to time. Whenever you are able to hear an inspirational speaker, I encourage you to take notes. Write down a few of the main points from the talk and keep those notes handy for a week. You will find that it will sink in and you will be able to keep your positive attitude!

Rick says that it's a crazy world and stuff happens. It doesn't make much sense, but you have to make the most of it.

What is something that has happened in your life that made no sense and maybe even was unfair, and how can you make the most of it?

— 39 —

Don't Mess with "Happy"

THE LATE JIM VALVANO used to have a saying, "Don't mess with happy." He was a successful college basketball coach who often was approached by other coaches for career advice. Many of them were looking to climb up the career ladder as high as they could and make the huge money. What Valvano meant was that, if you got to a job or place where you really liked it, why would you mess with happy?

I have been totally content and happy with my career choices because I always found my "happy." When I started out in television news, I had a lot of success and people assumed I would end up in a major market like Chicago or on ESPN since I was primarily a sports anchor. By age 25, I had already won three "Golden Microphone for Broadcasting Excellence" awards and had TV stations around the country very interested in hiring me. I remember at age 26 hearing about the opening for the sports anchor at the CBS station in South Bend, Indiana, a medium-sized market. I was intrigued because of the mystique of Notre Dame

Football and the legendary passion for Indiana high school basketball where 15 of the 16 biggest basketball gyms in America were located.

I accepted the job and soon found myself traveling quite a bit, covering Notre Dame as they played a national schedule. I would work out of the Los Angeles CBS newsroom for a few days when the Irish were in L.A. to play Southern Cal. I worked out of newsrooms in Dallas, Miami, New York City, and Phoenix. While I saw people who seemed pretty content, I saw many others who looked like they were not very happy. Sure, they were making more money, but the stress was evident. You could feel the pressure. I never will forget covering Notre Dame in the Orange Bowl in 1990 when they were playing the University of Colorado. We shared a work area with the CBS station from Denver. Those people were so stressed and ultra-competitive that I thought they were on the verge of nine heart attacks. They worked around the clock to "scoop" the other stations there. All of those experiences made an impression on me as I contemplated moving up the ladder.

At age 29, I was offered the sports anchor position at a station in New Orleans. It was there that I learned my "happy" was back in South Bend. I just did not care for the large-market mentality in TV news. Yes, I was making a lot more money, but the pressure was way higher! I also realized that I liked a medium-sized city. I despise being in traffic jams. That takes my positive attitude away in a hurry. In South Bend, I never had a traffic jam except for Christmas week near the local mall. So, after two years in New Orleans, I came back to South Bend and have been here ever since. I have so many memories here. It is where I fit. For you, it could be that you crave the kind of competitiveness that comes from larger environments. I have seen plenty of positive people who need to be in the most challenging environment. They thrive on it and would become negative and bored without it.

I was in TV news for 23 years and I LOVED going to work, especially in South Bend. My shift was from 2:30 to 11:30 p.m., but I would often go in an hour early because I couldn't wait to get to work. I loved Mondays! The key is finding your passion professionally and what God has gifted you to do. You also have to pay the price. When I was in college in student television news, I often worked 16 hours on Saturdays—covering a college football game and then driving up from Oxford, Mississippi, to a TV station in Memphis to edit three features until two in the morning that they would run the next week. Having that kind of work on my resume tape got me a job right after graduation and I was off to the races, working in Meridian, Mississippi, and then Bakersfield, California, and then South Bend.

After doing that for so long, I found that I was starting to wear out and that a new "fire" was burning within me. It was motivating groups and individuals to reach their dreams and goals through my motivational messages. I had been so blessed to interview thousands of peak performers in my television news days that, in 2005, I moved into professional speaking—specifically in the area of positive attitude. That has become my "happy" now.

While advisors have told me that I should speak mainly at high-level corporate events and command large fees, I don't do it. I keep my fees very reasonable because I like speaking to companies and organizations at all levels, not just the big shots. I like speaking to teachers and staff at schools and at small country churches. That makes me happy.

One of the reasons I have been able to build and keep a positive attitude is that I have been able to find my "happy" professionally (television news then professional speaking) and the right place to live (the medium-sized city of South Bend, Indiana). I have seen friends here up north crave to move south where it is warmer, but then they end up missing their extended family terribly, and almost always come back, because it is their "happy."

Take some time now to reflect on YOUR "happy." What would give you the most contentment professionally?

____

____

____

____

____

____

____

____

____

What have you done or are you doing to reach it?

What excuses do you have (violin music while you write this part)?

Write down what the ideal life for you would be, regarding where you live and what you do?

—40—

You Can Always Be Thankful for Something!

I WRITE A MOTIVATIONAL eNEWSLETTER and send it out across the world each Tuesday. If you would like to receive it, you can sign up for it at charlieadamsmotivation.com or send an email to charlie@stokethefirewithin.com.

One of the most well-received eNewsletters was the one I did on the positive attitude of a man named Kane Brolin. Kane has been blind since birth. He was born three months early at three pounds. He says they gave him too much oxygen in the incubator and that destroyed the part in the back of his eye that sends images. His response has been to "see" the positive in everything. "I can read in the dark [Braille] and walk around the house without the lights on!" he told me, with a smile. Now *that's* putting a positive spin on things!

He also looks on the positive by realizing Helen Keller couldn't see *or* hear. He *can* hear. He always emphasizes the positive in life. When Kane was a student at Iowa State University, his dad made him a wooden-frame map outlined with cloth, strings and glue to signify different places on campus. "I had very demanding parents," he said. "My father reviewed my school work. 'You have to do that over,' he would say. A lot of times I stayed up late doing the homework. It built values into me. I got my college education in Business. People trust me with their money."

Kane is an established financial planner.

"I have learned to be thankful for the ability to overcome things," he said. "Being blind is a characteristic. What's important is how you approach it." He says there are two things we can always do, whether facing a major health challenge or in a recession. "You can always have fun and you can always be thankful for SOMETHING!"

— 41 —

"Hey, How Are You?!"

HAVE YOU EVER THOUGHT about how often you say, "How are you?" during a day or how often someone asks you that same question? It's a lot! In some cases it could be twenty, thirty, forty or more times. In most cases we fire off an answer along the lines of "Doing pretty well, you?" Or we simply answer with "Fine."

Then there was the late Ed Friend (whom I wrote about in depth earlier in this book), a longtime policeman who was known for having one of the most positive-attitudes around. Every time I saw Ed and asked him how he was doing he would answer, "Delicious!"

That answer may not be for everyone, but you sure did remember it.

It is one thing to build a personal positive attitude and try to keep the darn thing, but why stop there? There are ways to help create an instant, positive-attitude environment. One way to interject a dose of positive attitude is to respond to "How are you?" with a positive response that can't help but make the space you're in more positive immediately! You can take the approach of having an answer for each day:

Monday: "I am marvelous!"

Tuesday: "I am terrific!"

Wednesday: "I am wonderful!"

Thursday: "Tremendous!"

Friday: "Fantastic!"

Saturday: "Super!"

Sunday: "Splendid!"

Here are some other ideas for when you are asked, "How are you?"

"Better than Good!"

"If I was better, I'd be twins!"

"Blessed!"

"Better than most. Not as good as some."

"I'm so happy I have to sit on my hands to keep from clapping."

"Pretty good for a young fellow!" (said to me by an 80-year-old man)

Having a positive answer like those above not only creates an instant positive atmosphere, it also rejuvenates your positive attitude. It helps you keep the darn thing!

What is going to be your answer to "How are you?" from this point on?

____

____

____

____

____

— 42 —

In Closing…

IT IS MY HOPE THAT YOU have taken away a lot of tools from this book to help you build and keep that darn positive attitude! As follow-up, I would love to come and deliver my "How to Build a Positive Attitude and KEEP the Darn Thing!!" seminars on the subject to your group. I have them structured in two-hour form so that I can do multiple ones during the day. In that way people from different shifts can attend one of the sessions. I can even stay over multiple days. I also have a half-day version of it, or I can deliver it in keynote form for your banquets, award sessions, and such. These work for corporate, association, school, college, and church groups.

I also have a keynote called "Stoke the Fire Within" that I have delivered everywhere from Juneau, Alaska, to Antigua and all points in between over the past two decades. "Stoke" is built to open conferences with a rip-roaring message tailored to the theme of the event. You can see video clips of it at charlieadamsmotivation.com.

Individually, I do coaching sessions in person or over the phone. I also have an experience where we spend a day at a location diving deep into your goals and what kind of attitudes it will take to make them come to realization.

I encourage you to come with me on one of the group inspirational trips I host for Edgerton's Travel each year. I share positive stories and lots of humor. Folks have come in from all over to be a part of these experiences. They are called "Travels with Speaker Charlie Adams." Since 2006, I have led groups to such locations as Alaska, Italy, Ireland, New Orleans, Charleston and Savannah, New York City, the California Coast and Wine Country, the Canadian Rockies, the Pacific Northwest, Hawaii, the Albuquerque International Hot Air Balloon Fiesta, Colonial Williamsburg, D.C. during Cherry Blossom Festival, Yellowstone and more. To have the brochures sent to you, simply call 574-256-2929 and ask for the Charlie Adams trips. You can also email Tom Edgerton, the owner, at tom@edgertonstravel.com .

I write on positive attitude each day on my Facebook and Twitter pages and write a weekly eNewsletter that you can subscribe to by writing:

charlie@stokethefirewithin.com.